Dorothy McRae-McMahon is a minister in the Uniting Church in Australia. For ten years she was a minister with the Pitt Street Uniting Church in the centre of Sydney and then for five years the National Director for Mission for her church. She was a member of the World Council of Churches Worship Committee for its Canberra Assembly and Moderator of its Worship Committee for the Harare Assembly. She now contributes to the Faith column of *The Age*, Melbourne and is a co-editor of *The South Sydney Herald*.

Her community awards indicate her interests and concerns. She has received a Jubilee Medal from the Queen for work with women in New South Wales (1977), an Australian Government Peace Award (1986), the Australian Human Rights Medal (1988) and an Honorary Doctorate of Letters from Macquarrie University in Sydney for work with minorities and her contribution to the spiritual life of the community (1992).

Also by the author:

Being Clergy, Staying Human
(Alban Institute, Washington, Australia, 1992)

Echoes of Our Journey: Liturgies of the People
(Joint Board of Christian Education, Melbourne, 1993)

*The Glory of Blood, Sweat and Tears: Liturgies for Living and
Dying*
(Joint Board of Christian Education, Melbourne, 1996)

Everyday Passions: A Conversation on Living
(ABC Books, Sydney, 1998)

Liturgies for the Journey of Life
(SPCK, 2000)

Prayers for Life's Particular Moments
(SPCK and Desbooks, 2001)

Daring Leadership in the 21st Century
(ABC Books, Sydney, 2001)

In This Hour: Liturgies for Pausing
(SPCK and Desbooks, 2001)

Rituals for Life, Love and Loss
(Jane Curry Publishing, 2003)

Liturgies for Daily Life

Dorothy McRae-McMahon

First published in Great Britain in 2004 by
Society for Promoting Christian Knowledge
Holy Trinity Church
Marylebone Road
London NW1 4DU

British Library Cataloguing-in-Publication Data
A catalogue record for this book is available from the British Library

ISBN 0-281-05694-3

1 3 5 7 9 10 8 6 4 2

Designed and typeset by Kenneth Burnley, Wirral, Cheshire
Printed in Great Britain by Ashford Colour Press

Contents

CONTENTS

Acknowledgements

I would like to thank MediaCom, Adelaide, Australia for its long-term encouragement of my liturgical writing, SPCK and its staff for all their help in editing and for trusting my work enough for publication, my agent Fiona Inglis of Curtis Brown, and the special people of the Uniting Church in Australia Parish of South Sydney for all they give to my life and faith.

Introduction

Liturgy, in my experience, is rarely created in mid-air. It arises from the ground in which its celebration is set. For me, the creative space for this liturgy is mostly in the Uniting Church in Australia Parish of South Sydney. This parish is set in possibly the most struggling area in Australia, with the largest urban Aboriginal population and a multicultural community in every sense of the word – people in public housing, people in tower blocks of apartments and terrace houses, people from many races, cultures and religions, old and young and rich and poor. There is a significant population of street people who are there for different reasons, like mental illness, poverty, abuse and addiction.

Our little congregation is perhaps the richest experience of the church I have ever had. Its life is raw, real and full of tears and laughter. I often think that if you can place the gospel on the ground among us and make it live, it will live anywhere. I will always remember our last Pentecost service. We were, as usual, seated around our communion table with its cross and the flowers that Juliette always collects for us and puts in front of the cross. Alongside the cross was the candle, which Fred lights for us each week, and the small candles waiting for our lighting when we bring our prayers of intercession. Vladimir Korotkov, our minister, was, with his usual earnestness, exploring in his sermon ideas about the absence and presence of God. We all listen because his sermons are worth hearing and because we usually get the chance to comment on his ideas – and some interesting comments there are too!

As we listened, we suddenly realized that what we were seeing in front of us was an amazing ray of light coming from above the gallery and slowly moving down on to the cross and Juliette's flowers. We stopped Vladimir's preaching and pointed it out in wonder as we received a sense of the gift of the Spirit of God among us. Then Vladimir continued and mentioned the dove of peace which descended on the disciples long ago and, as we watched in amazement, a tiny feather slowly spiralled from the high roof of the church and landed on the table in front of the cross. We all laughed and cried. We knew, of course, that we do have some pigeons living in the church roof, but we agreed that the timing and placement was a little miracle for us struggling, humble people in South Sydney.

When the gospel comes to people whose lives offer the hardest questions for life and God, it is hard won and it is either relevant or it dies. Worship becomes full of both greater pain and greater joy as people survive their next moments and laugh with delight at small victories for life and faith. We are the oddest collection of people and the life we share is full of gifts. Our services are often interrupted by people coming and going for all sorts of reasons and we receive those 'interruptions' as special opportunities.

We can hardly wait to tell each other when things go well or to hold each other when they don't. Our prayers of intercession are sometimes the longest part of the service. We have a Eucharist every Sunday – which is not common in our tradition – because we need to be reminded every Sunday that we are given the gifts of abundant life in Christ's body.

So this book is dedicated to my dearly loved friends at South Sydney Uniting Church, with grateful thanks for all that they give to me in life and faith.

Dorothy McRae-McMahon

Using these liturgies

Most of these liturgies would benefit by the inclusion of music. I have left it for the users to decide what music they will add and at what point. Music is a very cultural thing, even in the church these days. There are now very few 'well-known hymns' and sung responses!

When I am making suggestions about symbols or symbolic acts in a service, I have noted the main resources needed. However, I always assume that people add their own ideas in preparing the environment for liturgical events – that they will bring in their own cloths, candles, crosses, banners, contextual images or symbols, or anything else that might enhance the moment. I also assume that some people may prefer to take out the symbolic acts altogether and simply adapt the prayers.

When a liturgy has been specifically prepared around certain Bible readings, those readings are included, otherwise it is assumed that people will select their own as appropriate. Most of the services are prepared in relation to the lectionary readings from the Revised Common Lectionary. Having said that, some of the services which are attached to certain readings may well be used in other contexts and with other readings.

As a liturgist, I find that I pick up all sorts of ideas from other people and adapt them, revise them and develop them according to the context for my work. I assume that other people will do the same!

LITURGIES FOR HIGH DAYS

In the midst of the dead places,
in the heart of doubt and confusion:
Christ is risen!

On the ground where the bindings of life lie
in memory of our dyings,
grieving in the earth around our fears and our loneliness:
Christ is risen!

Before all that the forces of evil can deliver
and in the face of our betrayals and woundings:
Christ is risen in life and freedom!

Christist the King

CALL TO WORSHIP

We bow before your life, O God:
which holds the world into a plan of grace
that will never be defeated.

We bow before the Christ:
who lives your radical love,
with face turned towards a different royal dream.

We bow before your Spirit:
who shocks the universe
with the recreating, greening of life
in barren and burnt places.

On this day, we worship you, O God.

CONFESSION

Christ, the One who reigns over all the world,
we come in our smallness to make our confession.
We always have something which we acknowledge
falls short of your hopes for our life with you.
There is no time when we come
with clean hands and pure hearts,
when we look at the great vision to which we are called.
Remind us of the great hope to which we are called:
that we may follow the way of the cross behind you, loving
    Jesus.

We own that the suffering of the world is still there before us
and that we have not often responded to its weeping.
The homeless still seek for a dwelling place
in the courts of your temple, O God,
and the hungry still wait for their invitation
to share with us at the table of your feast.

3

The earth itself still struggles for survival, O God,
as we consume your creation
as though the resources which are there mean little
and were not intended for our children and their children's
   children.
Sometimes we find it hard to hope at all
as we work away at changing things for good
and see little for our efforts.
Remind us of the great hope to which we are called:
that we may follow the way of the cross behind you, loving
   Jesus.
Amen.

ASSURANCE OF PARDON

Come to the feet of God,
come to the holy mountain of hope and joy
and the valleys in which the Spirit lives in every age.
Grace waits for us, forgiveness belongs to us.
Let us receive it now and stand tall.
Amen.

READING

Ephesians 1.15–23
Matthew 25.31–46

SERMON

OFFERING

PRAYERS OF INTERCESSION

Dear God, show us your face in the strangers we meet.
We think today especially of these people:

The people bring their prayers for particular groups and places

Show to us your face, O God.
As we walk towards the celebration
of your coming into the world,
we pray that we will know you
and be your true friends today.

Even here, O God,
we know that there may be those among us
whose life cries out for comfort, healing,
justice or forgiveness.
Give to us your heart for knowing pain,
give to us your mind for wise and gentle care,
and give to us your strength for keeping the faith.
Show to us your face, O God.
As we walk towards the celebration
of your coming into the world,
we pray that we will know you
and be your true friends today.

This is our prayer for the coming days, O God.
Amen.

SENDING OUT

Go out in faith into the world,
for we are called to a great hope
which travels like a flame before us,
and which calls us on in the voice of the Loving Shepherd.

BLESSING

And may the reign of God be before our eyes
in colours of joy,
the feet of Christ walk ahead of us around every corner
and the Holy Spirit be an arm around our shoulders as we go.
Amen.

An Advent liturgy for use in hard times

Sometimes in the Southern Hemisphere, Advent is placed in an environment of drought. This liturgy was formed in response to the drought in many parts of Australia in 2002 but has been adapted for alternative use when times are hard in any sense. It holds together expectation and reality.

For this liturgy you will need

- *An Advent cloth on the table or flowing from the table on to the floor and down the central aisle*
- *A set of Advent candles*
- *Symbols for each Sunday in Advent: a Bible, some small candles, some wild berries and plants, rock or concrete and some blades of grass*
- *Small strips of gold ribbon or thread with safety pins attached in a basket on the table*

LOVE IS NEAR

CALL TO WORSHIP

The parched earth cracks and groans
under the blazing sun across the wide land,

and the trees droop in the hot wind
as we search the horizons for clouds
and wait for the cooler darkness.
**In faith and hope, we wait
in this time of Advent.**

After the suffering in these days,
the Child of God will be seen
deep in the heart of summer,
gentle in the centre of harshness,
and vulnerable in the midst of our vulnerability,
a frail but sure sign
of the promises of God.
In faith and hope, let us worship God.

OR

CALL TO WORSHIP

Wintry questions circle the earth,
in struggles for survival,
tinged grey with cynicism and apathy.
The dead leaves have lost their colour
and lie among white coldness on the earth
as the hearts of the people wait,
and wait for the spring.
**In faith and hope, we wait
in this time of Advent.**

After the suffering in these days,
the Child of God will be seen
deep in the heart of the winter,
gentle in the centre of harshness,
and vulnerable in the midst of our vulnerability,
a frail but sure sign
of the promises of God.
In faith and hope, let us worship God.

LIGHTING OF THE ADVENT CANDLE

First Sunday in Advent:
We light this candle as a sign
that heaven and earth may pass away,
but the word of God will be present in the world
for ever and for ever.

The candle is lit and the Bible is placed

Second Sunday in Advent:
We light this candle as a sign
that among the locusts and wild honey,
in the wilderness of life a sure voice rises,
calling us on to prepare the way for our God.

The candle is lit and weeds and berries are placed

Third Sunday in Advent:
We light this candle as a sign
that in the darkness of the struggle for life,
the light is surely coming,
the light for all the world in every generation.

The candle is lit and a circle of small candles around it

Fourth Sunday in Advent:
We light this candle as a sign
that God conceives and creates in barren places,
that new life will arise within the empty wombs of life,
for nothing is impossible with God.

*The candle is lit and a symbol of surviving life is placed, such as
a fragile blade of grass between concrete or rocks.*

CONFESSION

O God, as we enter the season of Advent, the waiting time,
we confess that there are many things about our own life

and the life of the world
which test our faith in your coming in love.
When the struggle in our own lives overwhelms us:
Come to us in grace, O God.

When we can only think of violence as the path to peace
and our trust in the possibility of human community wears thin:
Come to us in grace, O God.

When we feel that the universe itself is challenging your grace
and your word is hard to find:
Come to us in grace, O God,
for we are your humble people on a hard journey.
Amen.

ASSURANCE OF PARDON

Nothing can separate us from the love of God in Christ Jesus,
neither the emptiness of the land nor the droughts of the soul.
The Christ will come,
even when there seems to be no room
and no place prepared.
Grace is ours, love will come to us and to all humankind.
Thanks be to God.

THANKSGIVING

When life seems hard, we give you thanks for unexpected things:
gifts which arise in tough places from people who have little,
surprising sharing which did not seem to be there
until we all had less than before,
community which deepens in the face of need,
faith which is born in nothing but hope
and the age-long testimony of your faithfulness, O God.
Thanks be to you, Jesus Christ,
Thanks be to you, Holy Spirit and great Creator,
who is making all things new.
Amen.

READINGS

SERMON

SIGNS IN THE WAITING

In response to the word,
let us look for signs of love which are already among us.
Let us name some of those signs
and pin a golden ribbon to the Advent cloth,
a golden glimpse of summer,
to remind us of the hope that already lies here.

The people do so

AFFIRMATION OF FAITH

When the star-sign shows weak
above the blinding lights of the city,
it will hang low and bright
over the waiting landscape of desert and farmland:
The Christ is coming in love for all the people.

When the shepherds wait in faith in the fields,
the songs of hope will sound forth
from the gathered choirs in the streets in the distance,
sharing the gifts for now and the gifts to come,
in the spirit of the One who is near:
The Christ is coming in love for all the people.

We will prepare the way,
opening wide the doors of waiting stables,
dressing them in compassion,
carrying the remnant flocks in our arms,
holding them firmly in hope stretched thin.
We will prepare our gifts as the wise ones of old,

making ready to carry them
to the places where the Christ-child is unexpectedly born.
The Christ is coming in love for all the people.
The summer of Christmas is near.

OFFERING

PRAYERS OF INTERCESSION

O God of hope and bearer of peace,
we remember before you this day
those who most long for love to be born among them,
those near to us and those far away.

The people pray

Do not leave us comfortless, O God.
Send to us the signs that the waiting will not be for ever.

Point us to the tender greening of new life,
the fragile signs of our survivals,
the small watery trickles of things to come.
Send to us the signs that the waiting will not be for ever.

Transform the fires of our burning
into gathered care for all who grieve and suffer loss,
tiny candles lit beside the manger which carries your life.
Send to us the signs that the waiting will not be for ever.

Come into our world, Jesus Christ,
come and lead us on into the ways of peace and grace,
come and be the summer of the earth,
which brings fruitfulness and the miracle of new life.
Send to us the signs that the waiting will not be for ever,
for we pray in faith,
Amen.

SENDING OUT AND BLESSING

Go in trembling hope to point to the signs of love.
Go in peace, for God will not fail us.
And may the star-light of the heavens bring promises each night,
the signs of coming life be near our feet as we walk
and the hand of God reach out in all the earth
for the creation of a new future.
Amen.

Christmas Day (1)

CALL TO WORSHIP

On an ordinary night,
among people like us;
in an ordinary place,
with homes and streets for living and walking;
in a moment in time
when the stars wheeled across the skies
as they do now,
and sheep grazed in the grass
as they did each day:
All the earth received its Christ.

Christ, the one who came in the silences
amid the singing of angels,
the one who would never leave us nor forsake us,
born of a woman and offered to us all.
Let us celebrate Christmas,
God with us.

INVOCATION

As we pray that we may know your presence with us today,
O God,

we claim with joy the Christmas news that you have already
come to us.
Without our knowing, without our invitation,
you are the God with us who chooses to be in the midst of our
earthly life.
We pray that this Christmas Day we may know your presence
more fully.
We welcome you with thankful hearts, Jesus Christ.
Amen.

CONFESSION

God, who arrives as the vulnerable One,
we confess that the mystery of your presence often eludes us.
Were you here among us as the first peoples of this land
in other naming and imaging of the Divine presence?
Are you abroad, among those
whom we do not recognize as your people?
If we have ever destroyed the first-born creativity of those other
than ourselves
as though they threaten your existence:
Forgive us and give to us a great new vision of your birthing.

God, who comes among the singing of the heavens
and gifts of gold, frankincense and myrrh,
if we have created a dull and joyless place
in which we hope the people might find you:
Forgive us and give to us a great new vision of your birthing.

God, who is born from the womb of one of us,
who smelt the hay and the animals in your first resting place,
if we have enshrined you in our sanctuaries,
separating you from our earthy life:
Forgive us and give to us a great new vision of your birthing.
Open our hearts and souls to the marvel of your dream
of relationship with us and all people.
Amen.

ASSURANCE OF PARDON

Jesus breaks through all our defences of guilt and pain and
    grieving
with showers of graciousness.
On this Christmas Day, receive the forgiveness of God.
Join the heavenly hymns of thanksgiving and hope.
Grace has come into the world.
Thanks be to God.

THANKSGIVING

Hallelujah! Hallelujah!
The Christ has come!
Thanks be to God whose peace breathes new life
into the universe and into each heart
with love that will never cease or be defeated.
Thanks be to God!
Amen.

READINGS

Isaiah 62.6–12
Psalm 97
Titus 3.4–7
Luke 2.1–7 (8–20)

SERMON

OFFERING

PRAYERS OF INTERCESSION

As the flowers emerge in the desert after small drops of rain,
raise up new beauty and possibilities

in those whose lives seem too barren
for the celebration of Christmas, O God.

Silent prayer

As the stars hover over our land with delicate light,
bring the mystery of your comfort
to those who live with loss today, O God.

Silent prayer

As the sheep gather under the shade of the gum trees,
sheltering in their grey-green grace,
and the blue haze of eucalyptus-laden air rises in its healing
in the hills above our cities,
move into the struggling spaces among us, Jesus Christ,
Child of God, Prince of Peace, Very God of Very God.

Silent prayer

OR (for the Northern Hemisphere):

As the sheep gather into warm barns,
sheltering in the care of faithful shepherds,
as the cold air rises in cleansing rushes of energy
and the renewing rains fall
above the heart of our cities,
move into every part of our struggling life, Jesus Christ,
Child of God, Prince of Peace, Very God of Very God.

Silent prayer

Give melodies to our hearts and voice for the music of joy,
that those around us may see the miracle of love,
and the thankfulness of those who celebrate the God made flesh,
the one who dwells here in this day and every day.
Laugh in the delight of innocent hope,
little Christ-child,
when our life-denying cynicism overwhelms us.
Dance in the skies like clouds of angels,
winging their celebration above us

in the face of our lack of faith,
**God of breathtaking dreams.
For this is the day of days,
the day of Christmas.
Hallelujah! Hallelujah!
Amen.**

SENDING OUT

Go in peace. Go in grace.
Follow the stars of wonder and hope
as they shine on the pathway before us.

BLESSING

And may the love of God unfold before our eyes,
the light of the Spirit shine round our way
and the Christ be met in those we meet
and in ourselves.
Amen.

Christmas Day (2)

CALL TO WORSHIP

The earth holds its breath
as the Christ touches the ground of its life,
as God is placed among hay and wood,
among cities and bushlands,
among working and sleeping,
among pain and joy,
among beginnings and endings.

The earth holds its breath
as the waters of the birthing of love
are mingled with blood and courage,
the eternal signs of the bearing of costly life.
The earth holds its breath,
and so do we,
as we enter the moment of Christmas.

INVOCATION

Show us the marks of your feet among us, O Christ.
Touch us with your vulnerable child-like presence.
Take us into places of new birth which we have long forgotten,
that you may be real in this place,
the sacred known here,
and the divine stand in truth among us.
Amen.

CONFESSION

God in Christ,
God of Christmas Day,
if we have lost that sense of wonder,
if we have given Christmas away to our children
as though we have outgrown its stories,
if we have let the old words and carols flow over us
with little excitement:
Fill our barren souls
with the fullness of your surprising life, O God.

If we have been overtaken with our efforts to celebrate
and exhausted the reasons for the celebration,
relieved that it will soon be over
and a newer year to come:
Fill our barren souls
with the fullness of your surprising life, O God.

If we are overcome by losses and betrayals,
empty of innocent hope,
lacking in love and the surrounding care
which makes Christmas real:
Fill our barren souls
with the fullness of your surprising life, O God.
Lift up our hearts with delight
in the power of your Holy Spirit.
Amen.

ASSURANCE OF PARDON

The Word is born among us!
Christ is come among us
and nothing can separate us from the love of God.
Grace and peace is the gift to us this day.
We are forgiven.
Amen.

THANKSGIVING

Loving God, we have less than the voices of angel choirs,
but we lift our songs of praise to you on this Christmas Day.
Our prayers of thanksgiving rise with melodies of gratitude
that can never really express our wonder
that you would join us in the treading of our life,
that you would be of us and for us in this way.
We thank you for being God made real to us,
for being God held closely to us.
Amen.

READINGS

Isaiah 62.6–12
Psalm 97
Titus 3.4–7
Luke 2.1–20

SERMON

OFFERING

PRAYERS OF INTERCESSION

Come, Holy Child, and visit our world with your hope.
Where wonder and mystery have grown old and frail:
bring the brightness of your arrival.

Where bitterness and war have wounded your world:
bring the healing of your new dream for peace.

Where suffering and oppression have overpowered justice:
break into the centres of despair with your determined life.

Where there is emptiness and loneliness:
hold the hands of the people within your hands
and bring your love near to their tears.

Especially we remember today, these people and places:

The people pray

Because you have come, Jesus Christ,
we believe that there is no place which is far from the love of
    God,
no person who is less than another,
no situation which is not subject to your grace and hope.
On this Christmas Day,
we commit ourselves to carry your vulnerable life
into the world which you so love,
and to join the song of joy which rings down the ages
as those who have been touched by your life
celebrate your coming.
Amen.

SENDING OUT

Go into all the world as the Christ has come
with joy and hope for all people!
Lift high the life of Jesus in all that we are and do.

BLESSING

And may the star go ahead of us towards the Holy Child,
the night be filled with the sound of singing
and the morning bring the hush of peace on earth.
Amen.

Transfiguration (1)

Mystery on a mountain

For this service you will need

- *A large candle*
- *A good length of shining cloth*
- *A number of small candles and a taper*

CALL TO WORSHIP

God, who comes to us in the mountains of our life,
transformed and transforming holy presence,
shining through the valleys of our being,
warming and lighting our souls
with shining hopes
and awesome possibilities,
we praise you for the light of Jesus Christ.

A candle is lit

This is a new day:
At this time of new beginnings,
we come with hope for fresh ways of seeing your life among
     us
and our own lives.
We come to worship you.

The shining cloth is spread from the table

CONFESSION

Holy God, we are sometimes tempted
to believe that we can bring you down
to our own limited understandings of divine life.
Sometimes we try to capture you and define you,
so that we can show others that you belong to us.

Silent reflection

Jesus Christ, forgive us.
Remind us of your Godliness and our humanity.

God of great beauty,
sometimes we have reduced you to grim rules,
which seem important,
and have forgotten the grace-filled miracle of your presence
with its offerings that take us well beyond where we have ever
     been.

Silent reflection

Jesus Christ, forgive us.
Remind us of your Godliness and our humanity.

God of wonder,
if we have limited the riches of your love for us and all creation,

21

refusing to set foot on the soaring mountains of life in the Spirit:
Jesus Christ, forgive us.
Remind us of your Godliness and our humanity,
on this and every day.
Amen.

ASSURANCE OF PARDON

Jesus Christ springs free in risen life before us.
Here, in this place,
there is a mountain-top gift of grace for us.
In Christ we are forgiven.
Rise up and live!
Amen.

READINGS

Exodus 24.12–18
Matthew 17.1–9

SERMON

THANKSGIVING

Let us reflect on times when we have seen the wonder of God
and the faces of people in which we have seen glimpses of the
    Christ.

Silent reflection

If you wish to do so, come and light a small candle
and name the place or the person as you place it on the shining
    cloth.

The people do so

We thank you, God, that we can be lifted into wonder,
that you are not a boring, dreary God
who simply offers us laws on tablets of stone,
but one who carries us down the mountain
with breathless tales of more than that
and of things which are beyond words.
We thank you for miracle and mystery,
for spirit and truth.
Amen.

OFFERING

PRAYERS OF INTERCESSION

God, whose glory spreads across the skies of the universe
and deeply into human hearts,
we pray that you will renew, in us and in all people,
a sense of mystery and wonder
which restores the magic of life.
Place the bright white light of your startling truth
around the things we thought we knew,
so that we may rise up in surprise
and marvel at the dimensions of the faith to which we are called.

A silence is kept

Then, O Christ, turn us around to go down into the plains of life,
where people despair and become cynical,
where people suffer and lose sight of anything good,
and where people look at each other and see little of worth.
Place the light of your life around us all,
that we may see each other transfigured by your love for us.

A silence is kept

Come to us this day, O Jesus,
for we long to meet you.
Amen.

23

SENDING OUT

Walk free into the clouds which cover the mountains of life,
and discover our God waiting in a mystery of grace and love.

BLESSING

And may Jesus Christ stand before you in joy,
God the loving Parent of us all speak from overhead
and the Spirit hold your hand as you enter the life
which lies spread out below.
Amen.

Transfiguration (2)

The mystery of God

CALL TO WORSHIP

Holy, holy, holy God,
God of beauty and vulnerability,
God of the mountain tops and human plains of life,
God in the silences and the music,
in the stillness and the sweeping winds of truth,
God who is and ever will be,
we come to worship you.

INVOCATION

Dear God, we long to see with our own eyes
your transformed and transforming presence.
We know that we can only catch glimpses of your holiness,
like sparks of light in the centre of the many colours of our
questions,

or small comforting coolnesses in the heart of our angers and
    woundedness.
Be with us in the ways of your choosing today
as we remember the time
when you stood on the mountain with your friends.
Amen.

CONFESSION

God, in Jesus Christ, we come to you as people
who sometimes like to dismantle mystery
until it loses its gifts of wonder.
Sometimes we can't resist trying to hold it in our hand
and explaining it out of existence, O God.
Sometimes we change mystery into mundane facts
which conform to the limits of our understanding.

Silent reflection

Forgive us, God of all possibilities.
Forgive us and enlarge our souls.

If we have hardly dared to stop our striving,
in case we encounter you in a new way
or because we are busy trying to earn our salvation,
stop us now and call to us to wait and see you.

Silent reflection

Forgive us, God of all possibilities.
Forgive us and enlarge our souls,
show us your grace,
show us your holiness,
we pray in your name,
Amen.

ASSURANCE OF PARDON

The Christ has descended into the depths of our longing.
We are known and loved even in our failures.
Open your hearts to the love of God.
We are forgiven.
Thanks be to God.
Amen.

READING

Mark 9.2–9

SERMON

PRAYERS OF INTERCESSION

Loving Jesus, even as we see your majesty,
you invite us to live with all those
who walk their ways on the plains of life.
Lead us down from the heights of your presence, O God,
that we may find it more truly in other places.
Challenge our dim vision with the splendour of your own.
Lift our faith in the creative power which you place in our hands
and your power for healing and change.

A silence is kept

As we meet in this sanctuary,
bring together your prophetic ministry
and the mystic light of your holy face turned to the world.
Place in our hearts and prayers those who you hold in care this
day:

The people pray

O God, give us the resources we need to be your people
who take your grace to these for whom we have concern.
We pray too for your church:

The people pray

Free us to enter into the mysteries which lie in your life,
venturing in faith into places of your glory
which we have never visited,
and send us out to tell the story of all that we have seen
in a day which hungers for more than what we can buy or
    contain.
Be with us, we pray, O God,
Amen.

SENDING OUT

Go among the ordinary with the shining faces
of those who have seen the Christ in a new way.
Go in faith and hope.

BLESSING

And may every mountain ring with the sound of Christ's name,
every plain be spread out to receive the holiness of God
and the seas rise and fall in waves of joy.
Amen.

A liturgy for Lent (1)

Going down deeply into our lives

For this service you will need

- *A candle to be lit*
- *A cross*

CALL TO WORSHIP

God, who lives in the depths of the universe:
We worship you.

God, who calls to us in the depths of our hearts and souls,
joining in our weeping and our laughing,
full of kindness in the deep silences of our painful places,
speaking into the anxious centre of our struggles:
We worship you this day.

SYMBOLS OF THE LENTEN JOURNEY

We light this candle as a symbol of this part of our Lenten journey,
which is always lit by the light of Christ.

The candle is lit

We place the cross down low on the cloth
as a symbol of the costly love of God which lies
beneath and within all of life,
even at the end point of our hopes and faith
as we try to survive in the deep waters of life.

GRIEVING

Dear God, as we enter the journey towards Easter,
the invitation into a time of reflection,

we grieve our human failures
as we face some parts of our lives.

Silent reflection

Here, in this time of following you, the Christ,
down into the realities of who we are
and what we do or fail to do,
we know that we can never earn the costly grace
which you offer to us.

Silent reflection

Stay with us here, loving Jesus.
Stay with us,
even as we know the truth about ourselves,
for we ask it in your name,
Amen.

ASSURANCE OF PARDON

The word to us in Jesus Christ
is that we are never left alone, never condemned or rejected.
The Holy Spirit, healer, companion and comforter, is our friend.
We are forgiven.
Thanks be to God.

READINGS

SERMON

PRAYERS OF INTERCESSION

Gracious God, there is no one who goes unnoticed
as you tread the road with us.
Bring to our prayers for others your eyes of wisdom and care:

The people pray

God, who leads us on,
may we see the world as you see it
and carry us into deeper waters of concern.
**Show us ways of hearing the cries of the people
and move us to justice and compassion.**

Show us ways of touching the lives of people in this place
which take us deeper into relationship and celebration.
**And then, dear God, be our company
as we dare to enter our own lives.
Invite us to change and grow
in fullness of life and grander faith.
Make this year's Easter journey
one which we enter in Spirit and in truth.
Amen.**

OFFERING

COMMISSIONING

Go into the world as those who move faithfully
into the depths of life,
and who invite others to come with us.

BLESSING

And may God the Creator be a safe, strong rock below you,
Christ Jesus hold your hand as you go
and the Holy Spirit part the waters as you step into the river.
Amen.

A liturgy for Lent (2)
Journey into life

For this service you will need

- *A large candle and means of lighting it*
- *A mauve cloth, preferably cotton for easy writing*
- *Felt pens in a basket*
- *A basket of small objects for people to choose from, e.g. flowers, stars, stones, bright pieces of ribbon, heart-shaped objects like buttons, small crosses*

OPENING SENTENCES

The journey into life
is a choice which we make.
It is a choosing to follow the Christ
along passages of emptiness
and pathways of fullness,
through valleys of our fear
and along roadways of our faith,
gathering around us the love of God
for our safe travelling,
the courage of this Jesus
and the truth that the Holy Spirit will never leave us.
We also claim the wonder and grace of each other.
Thanks be to God!
We will travel together on the journey into life.

The candle is lit

CONFESSION

We thank you, O God,
that Jesus was tempted to turn away
from your calling to him to face the pain

which stood between him and risen life.
We are often tempted to do the same,
and we find ourselves failing to hold the ground
in the journey into fuller lives for ourselves.

Silent reflection

Forgive us, O God.
Be gracious to us, Jesus Christ.
Come to us in love and call us on again.

Then sometimes, O God,
because we cannot find a way forward for ourselves,
we are unable to stand firm for the good of others.
We stand and watch as their life is denied
because we lack energy, or courage, or commitment.
Forgive us, O God.
Be gracious to us, Jesus Christ.
Come to us in love and call us on again.
We pray in your name,
Amen.

ASSURANCE OF PARDON

Jesus Christ has already gone ahead of us,
paving the pathway to life with forgiveness
and sowing the seeds of hope to blossom on the way.
Grace is ours!
Thanks be to God.

READING

SERMON

WORDS FOR THIS WEEK OF LENT

Insert appropriate words for each Sunday according to the readings

Lent 1:
The heavens are opened and we can see
that God has sent the beloved child, Jesus,
to walk with us on the journey into life.
The reign of God has come near to us.

Lent 2:
Let us stand behind Jesus as we journey,
for Jesus will help us to turn our minds
towards abundant life,
even when the way is hard.

Lent 3:
Take out of life the things which oppress the people.
Take out injustice and exploitation,
take out greed and lack of compassion,
for these will always stand as barriers
on the journey into life.

Lent 4:
God so loves the world that we are not condemned.
We may travel safely in our humanness,
surrounded by a cloud of understanding and love,
for Jesus, our God, walks kindly with us.

Lent 5:
And what should we say as we see
that life lies the other side of pain?
Should we ask for an easier path?
We may well do that, O God,
because we are not Jesus.
But deep within us we know that true life still lies
beyond the times of pain,
and the light of your costly life
shines through the pain towards us.

Palm Sunday:
This is the day of hope in our own life with God.
This is the day when we know
that sometimes we are the ones who make the pathway for life,
so that hope and love and justice
can be cheered on in its tough journey.
This is one day when we take our stand.

CLAIMING COMPANY FOR THE JOURNEY

What person or belief is our hope and support?
Let us create a cloth which tells the story of that company.
Let us write on the cloth the names of people,
or the insights from God or each other,
which travel with us today.

The people write on the cloth

PRAYERS OF INTERCESSION

Who will we pray for today?
Let us name them,
and take one of the beautiful symbols in the basket,
which reminds us of the precious life in them.
Let us hold that symbol in our hand while we pray
and then place it among all that we find supportive
for the journey into life.

The people pray and place their symbols on the cloth

God be with us and all for whom we pray:
God be among us,
God be beside us,
God go before us,
and God stand behind us,
for you are the way, the truth and the life,
for ever and for ever.
Amen.

OFFERING

SENDING OUT

Go in hope as the people of God.
Go in faith into the journey towards Easter Day.

BLESSING

And may the streets of the city be pathways to life,
the Christ be discovered in those we meet
and the Holy Spirit guard us and keep us.
Amen.

Good Friday

For this service you will need

- *A long cloth flowing from the communion table*
- *A basket of flowers*
- *Small candles for lighting*
- *A bowl of sweet-smelling spices*

CALL TO WORSHIP

'I am he,' says the Christ,
and we step back.

A silence is kept

The truth stands before us in all its vulnerable, sacred life,
and we have nothing to say.

A silence is kept

The cup of costly death is taken in suffering grace,
and our hearts know a deep and wordless pain.

A silence is kept

This is our God.
Let us worship God.

INVOCATION

O Jesus Christ, on this day of all days,
we almost fear to invite you to show your face among us.
What if we see its pain and its dignity?
What if we know who we are in ways which are more than we
    can bear?
And yet, in shaking faith, we do pray that we will find you here
    today,
in all your awesome truth, in all your authentic life.
For this is Good Friday, the gospel for all the world.
Amen.

CONFESSION

Dear God, whose grace still hangs before all history,
if we have come to find you with our weapons as well as our
    lanterns and torches,
pretending to be searching for you
even as we set out to betray the love for which you stand:
Forgive us, Jesus Christ.

If we would rather warm ourselves before the fires of approval
instead of owning our friendship with you,
telling ourselves that we will wait for another day to be brave:
Forgive us, Jesus Christ.

If we sometimes carefully avoid being defiled,
rather than standing beside those who are rejected as unclean by
    others,

as though that is true holiness:
Forgive us, Jesus Christ.

When our own lives become too challenging,
and we are tempted to say, 'Away with him,'
rather than defending your life:
Forgive us, Jesus Christ.
For we are still your weak and failing disciples
and in need of your costly love.
Amen.

WORDS OF ASSURANCE

The word to us in Jesus Christ is that not one of those
who is given into the hands of God is lost.
Even the faithless, even the fearful, even the weak,
are carried into the love of God as they stand in humble
    confession
before the cross which holds the transforming life of God.
We are indeed forgiven.
Thanks be to you, O Jesus Christ!
Amen.

THANKSGIVING

There are really no words which can express our thanks to you,
    O God,
on this day of remembering your dying.
We thank you for walking so profoundly in our life that you do
    not avoid
our capacity for destroying that which is good and loving.
We now believe that you understand the risks we take in trying
    to live our life,
never able to enter it in courage and faithfulness as you do,
but given a hope in trying to tread in your footsteps.
Thank you, God of endless grace.
Amen.

READINGS

Isaiah 52.13—53.12
Psalm 22
Hebrews 10.16–25
John 18.1—19.42

SERMON

HYMN

OFFERING

PRAYERS OF INTERCESSION

Dear God, like Joseph of Arimathea we come, not very bravely,
to share with you in the cherishing of the truth in our day.
Here, we place around those whom we see defending justice and
    compassion
the signs of our recognition and honouring and we pray for
    them.
We pray for those we see around the world who take their costly
    stand for others:

*The people bring their prayers and a sign of cherishing – candles
or flowers or sweet-smelling spices sprinkled on a length of cloth
laid out from the communion table*

Stand with them in truth in our day, Jesus Christ.
Walk before them in hope and inspiration, O God.

We pray for those in our own country who invite us to look at
    the truth:

The people bring their prayers and a sign of cherishing

Stand with them in truth in our day, Jesus Christ.
Walk before them in hope and inspiration, O God.

We pray for ourselves, in our small hopes for witnessing to your
gospel:

The people bring their prayers and a sign of cherishing

Stand with us in truth in our day, Jesus Christ.
Walk before us in hope and inspiration, O God.

O God, the wonder is that, even in dying,
you speak to us in passionate ways
and call us on to new possibilities.
**Stay with us, Jesus Christ, Son of God,
who chooses to die rather than give up love.
Amen.**

COMMISSIONING

Go in peace.
This is not a day of endless grieving, but of hope for risen life to
come.
Go in faith,
for our God is faithful in all eternity and will not let us go.
This is the good news for the world,
the world which could become a new heaven and a new earth.

BLESSING

And may the pain of God become the glory of the gift of life,
the suffering of Jesus be the threshold to joy,
and the travail of the Spirit be the prelude to the miracle of the
birthing.
Amen.

Easter Day
Not an idle tale

CALL TO WORSHIP

In the midst of the dead places,
in the heart of doubt and confusion:
Christ is risen!

On the ground where the bindings of life lie
in memory of our dyings,
grieving in the earth around our fears and our loneliness:
Christ is risen!

Before all that the forces of evil can deliver
and in the face of our betrayals and woundings:
Christ is risen in life and freedom!
Let us worship God.

The Christ candle is lit

INVOCATION

Sometimes, even though we have come to find you,
our souls wander in lostness, O God.
We stand so close to you but do not know you.
We stretch out our longing hands towards you,
but do not find you.
Be revealed to us this Easter day, Jesus Christ.
Be known to us in the miracle of your victory over death.
Amen.

CONFESSION

Dear God,
in a world which often tells us that our faith is an idle tale,
we do sometimes find it hard to believe.
Forgive us and come to us, Jesus Christ.

So many experiences we have   .
seem to tell us that you have died:
the undeserved tragedies,
the power of destructive forces among us,
our own weakness in dealing with life,
and the unhealed people after we have prayed for healing.
Even our own stubborn independence of you when times are
    good,
and when we are tempted to depend on other things in our life,
make an idle tale of your rising, O God.
Forgive us and come to us, Jesus Christ.
Please do not be overcome by our sinfulness and lack of faith.
Amen.

ASSURANCE OF PARDON

Christ has died.
Christ is risen.
Christ will come again!
This is the promise, this is our faith.
Christ Jesus is indeed grace upon grace,
the One who dies rather than giving up love.
We are forgiven!
Thanks be to God.

READINGS

Acts 10.34–43
Psalm 118.1–2, 14–24
1 Corinthians 15.19–26
John 20.1–18

SERMON

HYMN

AFFIRMATION OF FAITH

In response to the word, let us affirm our faith:
It is the truth. Christ is risen!
The light of God burns in the world
in warmth and beauty
and in loving-kindness.
The truth of God is never defeated
as justice spreads its wings in hope.
Christ is never destroyed by our deaths of doubt,
but springs forth again in every generation.
This we believe, this is our faith,
for we have seen the life of Christ in our midst.

OFFERING

PRAYERS OF INTERCESSION

Risen God, life of the world,
we long to see the light of your compassion, your justice and
    peace,
in all the world.
Come, risen Christ, and bring your peace in a healing flow,
peace like a river of calm
into the conflict and wars of the world.
Come, risen Christ, and bring justice
like a burning fire of passion,
like a warm covering of right relationships
into the places where people are tortured,
starved, cold without shelter and clothing
or struggling for freedom.
Come, risen Christ, and bring love,
love like an all-pervading wind,
like a breath of compassionate touching,
moving into the places of hate and rejection,
loneliness and sadness.
Come, risen Christ, and transform us
as we share in the transformation of the world.
Amen.

SENDING OUT

Go in risen life:
find this life rising within us,
find this life rising among us,
and find this life spreading across the universe,
as God goes on recreating all that is
in every age and every place.

BLESSING

And may the air around you brush your face with gentleness,
the ground under your feet be like the rock of God's love
and the life of Christ be found in freedom before you.
Amen.

Pentecost

Spirit poured out

For this service you will need

- *A red candle*
- *A long red cloth*
- *Small tea candles*

CALL TO WORSHIP

See the cities' rising towers spiked with steeples:
and the Spirit of God poured out from heights to depths.

See the streaming fields of the countryside, with its dotted
     warmth of homesteads:
and the Spirit of God poured out from horizon to horizon.

See the passionate seas and the wonder of rocky variations on its
    shores,
see the bushland spreading its life into every spare place:
**and the Spirit of God poured out in eternal ripples and waving
of creative life.**
This is the day of celebration, the day of Pentecost!
Let us worship God.

INVOCATION

Our heads are bowed before you, Jesus Christ.
Send your Holy Spirit upon us this day as we wait in faith.
Surprise us again with the joy of your coming in this new way
    into the world.
Speak to us in our own language of life
and open our hearts, souls and minds to receive you.
Amen.

CONFESSION

Living God,
if we have lost the wonder of life in your Spirit
and cannot remember its passion and promise:
Forgive us,
and touch our souls with the flame of your life.

If we dare to believe that the Spirit speaks in only one language,
    which is ours,
and we no longer expect to find you
in people who are different and who have different ideas:
Forgive us,
and touch our souls with the flame of your life.

If one day has become like most others,
especially around our church,
and we are no longer expecting miracles:
Forgive us,
and touch our souls with the flame of your life.

44

When cynicism and lack of hope overcomes us
in the face of the realities around us,
shutting the door to the power of your Spirit in every age:
Forgive us,
and touch our souls with the flame of your life,
which burns for ever with love for the world and its peoples.
Amen.

ASSURANCE OF PARDON

The witnesses come to us down the centuries,
bearing their testimony to the grace of God,
the love of Jesus Christ and the communion of the Holy Spirit.
This is our salvation, this is our forgiveness.
Let us live by that faith.
Amen.

THANKSGIVING

We thank you, O God, that we are never left alone,
that even when the wilderness of life surrounds us in foreboding,
when the desert does not show its blossoms to us
and when the nights and days seem to hold nothing but hollow
    emptiness,
your Spirit is there in mystery and love,
recreating the life around us and within us,
so that we may live in faith again.
Amen.

READINGS

Acts 2.1–21
Psalm 104.24–34, 35b
1 Corinthians 12.1–13
John 20.19–23

SERMON

OFFERING

PRAYERS OF INTERCESSION

God, who comes to us and never leaves us in the Holy Spirit,
as we look at the way before us at this time,
with its needs and its weeping,
its possibilities and its challenges,
we will carry with us your gifts for our journey.

The red cloth is spread from the table and down the central aisle

Before you, we name some of the gifts we have received from
    you
as we try to be your people.
These gifts stand among us like small lights,
reflections of the flame of your Spirit.

*The people name the gifts, and light the small candles and place
them on the cloth*

Holy Spirit of God, giver of gifts,
these are our prayers for those who long for your comfort and
    justice:

The people bring their hopes and concerns

We pray that you will visit us with your salvation
and enlarge our lives to meet what lies ahead,
believing that your presence will be with us in every moment.
And now, we ask that you will pray for us,
bringing the prayers we dare not name or do not know.

A silence is kept

Stay with us, Spirit of Christ, Spirit of God,
For we will always need you on the way.
Amen.

SENDING OUT

Go into all the world as the people of the Holy Spirit,
gifted in a myriad ways, hearts lifted up in hope,
transforming everything we touch into signs of the love of God.

BLESSING

And may the life of the Holy Spirit fill our being
until it overflows with healing, peace, inspiration and courage,
and dances on before us in joy and faith.
Amen.

LITURGIES FOR
ORDINARY SUNDAYS

The world weeps,
but somewhere beyond our sight there is a dancing.
The creation groans,
but deep within its life there is still a singing.
Our hearts are empty of God
but suddenly Christ sits at table between us
and invites us to a feast of life.
Let us worship God!

Come and see

John 1.43–51

For this service you will need

- *A large candle*
- *Smaller candles and a taper*

CALL TO WORSHIP

Come and see the beauty of God,
life like the sudden gold of sunlight at dawn,
truth that breaks through as lightning flashes,
kindness like the rain after dryness
and caring springing up in unlikely places
in the centre of cities.
Come and see the holy God.
Let us worship that God.

CONFESSION

God of all eternity,
as we seek your face, show us who we are.
Visit us deeply in the life-places which we refuse to name.
Speak to us in the silences, O God,
where our words of guilt and regret lie unspoken
and listen in the spaces where our souls whisper in longing
for different ways of being.

Silent reflection

Forgive us, O God.
Lay your hands on our lives in grace, Jesus Christ.

As we stand before your holiness,
we know we will never be who we would like to be.

51

Our faith is too small and our faithfulness too brief,
our courage fails us and our care for others comes and goes.
We are often slow to point to you if it costs us something
or if it seems meaningless to do so.
Forgive us, O God.
Lay your hands on our lives in grace, Jesus Christ.
For we come in hope to you.
Amen.

ASSURANCE OF PARDON

Come and see the grace of God for us.
We are loved as we are, not as we believe we should be.
We are given forgiveness as a gift,
beyond anything we have deserved or earned.
Let us lift up our hearts and receive our freedom.
Amen.

THANKSGIVING

We thank you, God,
for the life which is offered to us in your word.
We thank you for its layers of meaning and truth
which we can see in fresh ways as the years pass,
or as different experiences turn the pages of life for us
and bring new gifts of understanding.
We thank you also for the word which comes to us today.
Amen.

READING

John 1.43–51

SERMON

COME AND SEE WHAT WE HAVE SEEN

Let us share things which we have seen
which remind us of the beauty and goodness of God
and light candles of celebration.

The people do so

PRAYERS OF INTERCESSION

O God, who waits for our prayers
and reaches out towards our hopes each day,
we pray for the world:

The people pray

Close the distances between us and the people for whom we
    pray.
Give to us your energy for good
and a new courage to announce your prophetic truth, O God.
Show us your activities in the world,
so that we may be encouraged.
Give us new faith when nothing seems to change
and the strength to go on.

We pray for your church:

The people pray

Light a flame for the warming of our witness
and the lighting of our pilgrim way, O God,
that those who long to touch your life
will find it here among us.
Give us an open door for those who live in loneliness
and gentle hearts for those who fear our judgements.

We pray for ourselves:

The people pray

Be with us wherever we are in our faith, O God:
in our vulnerability or our emptiness,
in our strength or our fullness.
Be with us, whether our needs are known or not
and give to us a deeper caring for each other.
There is never a time when we do not need you, O God.
Come, gracious Jesus, come.
Amen.

SENDING OUT

Go in peace.
Call to all the people, 'Come and see our God,'
the God of love and compassion.

BLESSING

And may our eyes see the signs of the wonder of God,
our ears hear the sounds of the Spirit calling us on
and our feet be placed in the footprints of the Christ.
Amen.

Questions and answers

Matthew 21.23–32

CALL TO WORSHIP

Lying under the heavy rocks of tradition
is the determined life of God.
Springing up in the most unlikely places
is the rebellious life of God.

Moving and flying and soaring
is the leaping energy of the life of God.
Let us worship God,
the one who lives in eternal freedom.

INVOCATION

Move within our life, O Jesus Christ.
Come to us with the authority of truth,
be with us in the beauty of wisdom.
Call us on into new ways of knowing you
and new faith in seeing where you might be,
among us and abroad in all the earth.
Amen.

HYMN

CONFESSION

God, who can never be defined by any of us,
we are sorry that we look for you with limitations in our minds,
with the careful drawing of pictures which fit our imaging of you,
like golden calves in our heads.
Bring your grace to our lives
in costly forgiveness, Jesus Christ.

When we label others as having no authority
in order to give weight to our own power,
dismissing what they have to offer as less worthy:
Bring your grace to our lives
in costly forgiveness, Jesus Christ.

If we say that we belong to you
and do little as the world waits and weeps in pain:
Bring your grace to our lives
in costly forgiveness, Jesus Christ.
Turn us around to face the real task and the real truth.
Amen.

ASSURANCE OF PARDON

Even our own foolishness is forgiven,
even our own self-righteousness
can be gathered into the heart of a hopeful God,
and love is given in ways beyond our understanding.
We are forgiven!
Thanks be to God.

READING

Matthew 21.23–32

SERMON

HYMN

PRAYERS OF INTERCESSION

Loving God, sometimes even our praying bears the marks
of our fenced-in views of the world.
Sweep across our hearts and minds and souls
with the winds of your Holy Spirit,
that we may blow apart our preconceived views
about who needs our care and your justice.
Expand our praying as we bring people before you:

The people pray

Remember all who struggle, Jesus Christ.
Gather them into your abundant life, O God.

Take the edges of our hopes and dreams
out towards your horizons,
so that they embrace people we have never seen
as belonging among us.
Remember all who struggle, Jesus Christ.
Gather us into your abundant life, O God.

Place your hands under your church
and lift us into heights of creativity and prophetic life
which speak daringly to the world,
calling into sound questions which lie unspoken,
and answers which break open
the way we live together
for the reforming of your gracious community.
Remember us as we struggle, Holy Spirit.
Gather us into your abundant life, O God.
We pray in the name of Jesus Christ.
Amen.

COMMISSIONING

Go in faith, carrying the deep questions among us,
and moving with the best answers we can find
as the Holy Spirit inspires us to truth.

BLESSING

And may God be in our knowing,
Christ Jesus be in our wondering
and the Holy Spirit lead us on towards a greater understanding.
Amen.

I do choose

Mark 1.40–45

CALL TO WORSHIP

God of miracles and gifts,
God of humanness and divine life,
God of unexpected connections with us
and mysteries of creativity far beyond our seeing,
God of the little and the least
and of those who think they are powerful:
You have chosen to be our God.
We have chosen to be your people
and we come to worship you.

HYMN

CONFESSION

O God, who lived our life with awareness and clarity,
we bring our confessions before you today.
We believe that you have chosen to know who we are
and to enter our every reality.
This is something we find hard to do ourselves.
There are times when we would rather not know who we are,
when we pretend to ourselves
and skip across the things we would rather not see.

Silent reflection

Give us faithfulness in facing all these things, O God.
Then choose to come and heal us in our need, Jesus Christ.

Then, O God, there are times when we would rather
give to others the choices about the world in which we live.

We decide that we have no power over systems and
    governments,
over economic forces and decisions that deeply affect people.
We tell ourselves that 'they' need to do something rather than us,
that we have little choice and little responsibility.

Silent reflection

Give us faithfulness in facing all these things, O God.
Then choose to come and heal us in our need, Jesus Christ,
for we are people of small faith.
Amen.

ASSURANCE OF PARDON

Reach out your hands and bow your heads in hopefulness.
The Christ comes to heal the people, even us.
We are forgiven and restored to the life which is our calling.
Receive all that God offers to us this day.
Amen.

READING

Mark 1.40–45

SERMON

HYMN

PRAYERS OF INTERCESSION

Come, Creator God, come to us.
Choose to enter the tiredness of our efforts in your name
with the energy of your creativity.

Choose to be present in our imagination,
our hopefulness or our frustrated waiting.
Choose to be strong in our fragile courage
and engaging in our every initiative.
This is where we long for your creativity today,
this is where we need to find your hand
stretched out in healing:

The people pray

Come to us, O God.
Come, Creator God, come to us.

Come, loving Jesus, come to us.
Come in the faithfulness of your understanding,
releasing us from condemning ourselves or condemning others.
Come in your earthly reality among us,
healing our wounds as we go
and teaching us new truth about life and God.
Come to us, O God.
Come, Jesus Christ, come to us.

Come, Holy Spirit, come to us.
Choose to sweep through our world
with the breath of your truthfulness,
showing us the lies and illusions which cloud our judgements.
Choose to give us the gifts of your wisdom
and the heart-lifting melodies of hope
which lie within your life.
Come to us, O God.
Come, Divine Spirit, come.
Amen.

SENDING OUT

Go into the world as those who choose and are chosen
to bring justice, peace and freedom to a longing people.

BLESSING

And may God be in our every action,
Christ Jesus be in every pausing to listen
and the Holy Spirit be in every moment of choosing.
Amen.

How then shall we live?

Matthew 16.21–28

CALL TO WORSHIP

There is a pathway of passion, of costly life,
which leads us towards the Christ
who always walks before us.
Call us on, Jesus Christ.

There is a company of the faithful
who have gone ahead,
singing with life in the Spirit.
Call us on, Jesus Christ.

God, the great Creator,
cups hands of love around us as we go.
Call us on, Jesus Christ.

COME, HOLY SPIRIT

There are times, loving God, when we know that
to acknowledge your presence among us
is to invite your challenge into our lives.
But still we do that in faith,
with our vulnerable lives only too clearly before you.
Come to us this day, Spirit of God, Spirit of Christ.
Amen.

HYMN

CONFESSION

God, who does not turn away from the truth about our life,
even unto death,
we confess that we have far less courage.
We often pretend to ourselves, we often pretend to others,
and sometimes we even try to pretend in your presence.
If we are afraid to see who we have become,
if we are too grieved about our lives to ask for forgiveness,
or if we are too proud to ask others for forgiveness:
Stand before us in the truth of your costly grace, Jesus Christ.

When our lives celebrate comfort and complacency
instead of the journey of faith,
when we close off the reality of the lives of others
because it demands a response we will not give:
Stand before us in the truth of your costly grace, Jesus Christ.
Speak into our hearts in new ways,
the ways of your faithfulness to us, O God.
Amen.

ASSURANCE OF PARDON

Even as we pray, the life of Jesus moves towards all that would
destroy us,
healing, loving and bringing grace.
We are forgiven!
Thanks be to God.

READING

Matthew 16.21–28

OFFERING

What can we offer to a God who gives us everything?
The good news is that God does receive our gifts,
so let us bring them now.

OFFERING PRAYER

Hold out your hands, God of grace, and receive all that we offer.
Take our lives, our love and all that we bring in faith today
and use us and our gifts for the well-being of the world.
Amen.

PRAYERS OF INTERCESSION

We pray that we will choose life, O God,
your life which lifts our eyes to a cross
on the pathway to risen life for all people
and ourselves.

Silent reflection

We pray today for all who long for freedom,
who wait on the edges
hoping that someone will see their pain,
and who reach out hands to your cross in hope or faith.
These are the ones we have seen before us
and for whom we now pray:

The people pray

We pray for ourselves,
your people of this day
who look with awe at the task in front of us,
as did the disciples of long ago.
We pray that we may be filled with your energy
for transforming the world,

and your courage in facing all that life brings,
whatever that may cost in sacrifice and love.
Give us all that we need to follow your cross in faithfulness.
We ask it in the name of Jesus Christ,
Amen.

COMMISSIONING

Go forth as those who have chosen
to follow the way of the cross with Jesus at your head.

BLESSING

And may the road stretch straight and clear before us,
the bread of life be in our hands
and the Spirit provide us resting places on the way.
Amen.

Mourning into dancing

John 21.1–19

CALL TO WORSHIP

The world weeps,
but somewhere beyond our sight there is a dancing.
The creation groans,
but deep within its life there is still a singing.
Our hearts are empty of God
but suddenly Christ sits at table between us
and invites us to a feast of life.
Let us worship God!

INVOCATION

In this homely place,
the every-week place of our coming together,
show us your face, O Christ.
Lift our hearts
so that we leap into the waters of life to meet you
and to take up the task of sharing in your vision for the world
and making it real.
Come to us not only now, O Jesus,
be there for us in every moment.
Amen.

CONFESSION

Sometimes, O God, risen in the world,
we are so busy fishing
that we do not see you on the beach preparing breakfast for us.
Sometimes we look and do not recognize you
because we have already decided what you will look like.
Forgive us and call us by our names, O God.

Sometimes we would rather not hear the weeping of others
because we cannot cope with what it would mean to care for
   them.
Forgive us and give us the courage to hear the pain of the
world, O God.

Sometimes we choose to stay mourning your death
because it is easier than joining your dancing.
We choose not to stay open to your healing and renewal.
If these things are true for us, O God:
Forgive us and lead us forth into the dance of life.
Amen.

ASSURANCE OF PARDON

The Christ comes in grace to the little and the least,
to the people of much faith
and to those who have lost hope about themselves.
We are all forgiven.
Come to the feet of Jesus Christ and find kindness.
The Christ is waiting to receive us.
Amen.

THANKSGIVING

Thanks be to you, O God,
for Jesus who came to the disciples in ordinary ways,
cooking and lighting fires,
talking about fishing
and walking on a beach.
We thank you that this gives us the faith
to watch for a meeting with Jesus,
on our beaches and by our meal preparations,
in our cities and towns and as we meet our friends.
Thank you, God, that you are not only a God of faraway places.
Amen.

READINGS

Acts 9.1–6
Psalm 30
Revelation 5.1–14
John 21.1–19

SERMON

OFFERING

PRAYERS OF INTERCESSION

O God, we know that much of the world is still in a state of
    mourning.
We look around at our life here and in faraway places
and we see the painfulness.
These are the places where we see the weeping, O God,
the places of hunger and suffering:

The people bring their prayers

Bring your healing, justice and peace, O God,
so that those who weep know that their tears are not in vain
and that somebody cares.
These are the people where we see the longing, O God,
the places of searching and confusion:

The people bring their prayers

Bring your wisdom and creativity, O God,
so that those who live in longing know that somebody
has met their anxious hearts.
These are the places where we see the sadness, O God,
the places where there is loss and loneliness:

The people bring their prayers

Bring the deep peacefulness of your joy, O God,
the covering of your warm hand of love and comfort,
that those who mourn know they are not alone.
**Hear our prayers for others and for ourselves, O God.
Amen.**

SENDING OUT

Go with songs of joy in your hearts.
Go with a dancing step into the world
for we are the children of the risen Christ,
the ones who are called into the wonder of God's life.

BLESSING

And may all creation lift up its heart in gladness around us,
the children of God emerge as a community of grace
in the light of our God, the God of risen life.
Amen.

Our sins are forgiven

Mark 2.1–12

CALL TO WORSHIP

Grace upon grace,
love which never ends,
honouring our human life:
Christ Jesus, God with us.

Kindness personified,
gentleness which goes beyond our understanding,
holding us like a parent:
God our Creator.

Comforter, healer, restorer and truth-giver,
the One always present:
Holy Spirit, Holy friend.
God in three persons, we worship you this day.

HYMN

INVOCATION

Be among us today we pray, Holy Spirit.
Come and enter our deepest life
so that we may find you there,
healing us before we know it,
sustaining our best life in our journey as your people,
at one with us,
touching us in truth like the breeze caressing the trees,
touching us in passion like the wind bending the boughs,
touching us in joy to bring the flowering of newness.
This we pray in faith,
Amen.

CONFESSION

Dear God,
sometimes we think it would be better
to sit in silence before you
rather than try to make our full confession.
There is no way in which we could really tell you
the full story of who we are.
Sometimes we do not even realize what we have done.
Often we believe that we are right and others are wrong,
without acknowledging that we can only ever act in faith.

Silent reflection

Forgive us, O God.
Look upon us with kindness and forgive us, Jesus Christ.

Sometimes, O God, we would be grateful
for friends who would carry us into your presence
and allow us to simply lie there and wait for you to know us.
We become paralysed in our attempts to face you in spirit and in
    truth.

Silent reflection

69

Forgive us, O God.
Look upon us with kindness and forgive us, Jesus Christ.

Then, O God, there are the times
when we refuse to forgive others who are genuinely sorry,
or we pretend we have forgiven them
but go on punishing them in subtle ways,
even as we pray to you for our own forgiveness.

Silent reflection

Forgive us, O God.
Look upon us with kindness and forgive us, Jesus Christ,
for we rely on your grace alone.
Amen.

ASSURANCE OF PARDON

Jesus Christ is the challenge
to the harsh judgements of the world.
Eternal grace is the gift which Christ brings to us,
time after time, to all sorts of people
in every place and stage of faith.
We are forgiven!
Thanks be to God.

READING

Mark 2.1–12

SERMON

HYMN

PRAYERS OF INTERCESSION

Dear God, we know that you forgive us in our failures
to transform the world into a place of love and justice.
We also know that your grace should create
such thankfulness within us
that we redouble our efforts to be your true people.

We pray today for the energy, courage and commitment
to be those who inspire greater and grander dreams
for the planet and for all people.
Especially we pray for these concerns, O God:

The people pray

Hear our prayers, O God.
We pray also for ourselves:
if we are grieving, touch our faces in comfort,
if we are worried, breathe into our hearts your peace,
if we are lost, find us and hold us fast.
Hear our prayers, O God.
Be alive in us,
be strong in us,
be gentle in us
and carry us towards your faithfulness.
Amen.

HYMN

SENDING OUT

Place your lives in the hands of God
and walk forward on the pilgrim way in faith.

BLESSING

And may the Holy Spirit light a flame of joy ahead,
the Creator celebrate our every growing moment
and Christ Jesus be our daily companion.
Amen.

The gift of eternal life

John 6.35, 41–51

For this service you will need

- *A candle*
- *A bowl of earth and some seeds beside it*

CALL TO WORSHIP

God who lives and breathes in all time,
all space, all histories, all things,
and all people in every age,
God of eternity:
We bow before you,
for we are ever your humble people.

Christ, Bread of life,
living witness to eternal life
in all its costliness and joy:
We bow before you,
for we are ever your humble people.

Holy Spirit, our company for ever,
leading us, guiding us in eternal faithfulness:
We bow before you,
for we are ever your humble people.
We worship you this day.

The candle is lit

INVOCATION

Come, O God, as a breath of eternity,
sweeping through our life
with the winds of truth and grace.
Touch us in ways which we recognize
in the midst of the things which distract us,
that we may know you again in every part of our life.
Amen.

HYMN

CONFESSION

Loving Jesus,
even as you promise us that we may share in eternal life,
we are tempted to keep that life for the future,
rather than honouring it in our life now.
It is so easy to imagine ourselves
participating in eternal life after death, O God,
instead of living with the hope of beginning it now.

Silent reflection

We confess that, even in the life of our country,
we are often tempted to see our responsibilities as short term,
good enough for our present agendas,
rather than as part of the grand sweep of the future,
your eternal future.

Silent reflection

Bread of life, feed us now.
Bring us your grace
and nurture in us the things of eternity,
we pray in your name.
Amen.

ASSURANCE OF PARDON

The grace of God is eternal and faithful.
There is no condemnation in the heart of God.
The love of God lasts for ever. We are forgiven.
Thanks be to God.

READINGS

Ephesians 4.25—5.2
John 6.35, 41–51

SERMON

HYMN

SIGNS OF ETERNAL LIFE

What do we see as signs of eternal life in our own community?
Let us place a seed in the bowl of earth
as we name those signs –
the beginnings of things which are growing among us
as gifts from the life of God.

The people do so

PRAYERS OF INTERCESSION

O God, we come in awe before you
to ask that you share our life
and the life of those for whom we are concerned.
We pray that you will be with us now
as we bring our prayers for others:

The people pray

We place these, who need your care,
before the eternity of your love, Jesus Christ.
Hold your hands beneath them and around them, O God.

Give us glimpses of the justice which is part of your eternity,
give us images of the breadth of your compassion,
give us touches of your power to transform all life, O God,
and signs of the healing which lies deep within your heart.
We place ourselves, who need your care,
before the eternity of your love, Jesus Christ.
Hold your hands beneath us and around us, O God.

Then we will see anew
the great hope to which we are called
and the faithfulness which encircles us
as we tread this journey.
We pray in the name of Jesus,
Amen.

OFFERING

HYMN

SENDING OUT

Go into all the world as the people of eternal life.
Lift high that life among the people.

And may the life of God be wide and deep among us,
may the universe witness to the wonder of eternity
and our every moment be a moment worth keeping.
Amen.

The sower and the seed

Matthew 13.1–9, 18–23

CALL TO WORSHIP

Listen with ears of hope.
Hear with ears of wisdom.
Learn with hearts of faith,
as we are moved by the word.
For God speaks to us now,
Christ calls us down the years
and the Spirit opens our minds and souls to the truth.
Let us worship God.

HYMN

CONFESSION

Dear God, who is imaged in Jesus Christ,
when we are tempted to look at the lives of others
as though they have the same opportunities as we do,
ignoring the differences in beginnings and endings,
in support and nurture,
in circumstances and levels of struggle:
Forgive us and open our eyes to the truth, O God.

If we fail to search our hearts about the things
which distract us and seduce us in this life,
things which take away our dependence on you
and divert us from the real journey of faith:
Forgive us and open our eyes to the truth, O God.

When we simply go on without thinking deeply at all,
treating one day like any other,
complacently choosing to avoid struggling
with the big questions before us:
Forgive us and open our eyes to the truth, O God,
and bring us before you in a new way.
Amen.

ASSURANCE OF PARDON

Even as we bring our confession before our God,
the commitment of costly grace still stands.
There is indeed no condemnation
for those who are in Christ Jesus.
We are forgiven!
This is the gift of God to us.
Amen.

READING

Matthew 13.1–9, 18–23

SERMON

HYMN

OFFERING

PRAYERS OF INTERCESSION

God, who so loves the world,
show to us the places and the people
who struggle on barren soil,
or who cannot put down the roots of faith
because life is too hard for the sustaining of hope.

Silent reflection

We bring our prayers for those
whom we have seen as needing your nourishing love:

The people pray

Give to us warmed hearts for understanding others, O God.
Give to us open minds to hear and interpret
the stories of people's lives,
and the strength we need
to respond in your name to the realities of our day.
For we would be the sowers of your good seed of righteousness
in all the world
and the tender carers of all your creation.

Silent reflection

Give us a new understanding of each other, O God,
as we live out the faith together.
Give us trust as we share our stories and truths,
give us mercy and kindness as we share our confessions.
May we be generous of heart,
honest in our humanness
and filled with your grace.
Amen.

HYMN

SENDING OUT

Let us go in faith, carrying the gift of wisdom with us.
Let us go in peace,
as those who bring good news into the world.

BLESSING

And may life in all its beauty and colour be spread before us,
and the roots of our faith grow deep into the earth around us
as a living testimony to the joy of the Holy God,
our Creator, Saviour and Friend.
Amen.

We are the branches

John 15.1–8

For this service you will need

- *A cross on the communion table*
- *A basket of cut flowers*

CALL TO WORSHIP

God in Christ is the victory,
the life which conquers the world:
the victory for love,
the victory for justice,
the victory for grace.
This is our faith,
born in a miracle of costliness.
This is our faith leading us on.
Let us worship our God.

HYMN

CONFESSION

God, who calls us to truth,
we acknowledge that our lives do not always blossom
with your fruitful life.
We often forget to cherish
the roots of our life with your word,
and we turn away from the grace which would restore us.
Forgive us, O God.
Nurture our living with your kindness, loving Jesus.

Sometimes we choose to go on in our own power, O God,
until our lives begin to wither in exhaustion.
Sometimes we occupy ourselves
with trivial issues and tasks,
pretending to ourselves that our life is productive.
We hide behind these things,
like canopies of covering leaves
which bear no real fruit.
Forgive us, O God.
Nurture our living with your kindness, loving Jesus.

We often find it hard to choose the larger life, O God,
the one which requires more courage and greater faith.
We rather choose to stop growing,
to stay as small plants,
fearing the tougher journey into maturity
and the rigour of wider, deeper life.
Forgive us, O God.
Nurture our living with your kindness, loving Jesus.
We ask this in your name,
Amen.

ASSURANCE OF PARDON

The true vine is the source of the renewal of our life.
Every time we come in faith, forgiveness is given to us in grace.
Let us claim our life in freedom and hope.
Amen.

READING

John 15.1–8

SERMON

HYMN

OFFERING

PRAYERS OF INTERCESSION

Dear God, even as we carry before us in faith
the hope that the victory belongs to you,
we are visited by doubts.
We pray for the lifting of our life this day
in new dreams for the future,
new visions of all that might be,
in a world where you have conquered the things of death.
May your creative power flower into fruitfulness
in the harsh deserts of our struggling life,
especially in these places.
Let any who wish take a flower and place it before the cross
as they pray for a particular hope in our life:

The people do so

May the roots of your faithfulness to the world
spread down deeply into all the earth,
that we may see the growing signs of your life in us
in every place.
Prune from our life all that is not needed,
all that does not bear fruit for the feeding of the people.
Then bless us with the company of Christ, O God,
in our laughter and tears,
in our wisdom and foolishness,
in our pain and in our joy.
Stay with us, loving Jesus,
this day and in the days to come,
as our saviour and our friend,
Amen.

HYMN

SENDING OUT

Let us go into the world
as part of the spreading life of God,
fruitful, faithful and in peace.

BLESSING

And may the life of God be in our beginnings,
the heart of Christ be at our centre
and the inspiration of the Holy Spirit shape all our endings.
Amen.

What matters most?

John 12.1–8

CALL TO WORSHIP

God expands our world,
stretching its boundaries into mystery and wonder,
calling us to go deeper and beyond,
shocking us into silences
as we remember our true centre
in the midst of life's complexities.
This is our God.
Let us worship God!

INVOCATION

Enter our hearts in this hour, O God.
Be made plain among all our theories of life,
and all our interpretations of your way.
Stand clear in our souls so that our lives reshape themselves
into your clarity, your priorities and your wisdom.
Challenge our sureness, break open the truth.
Be known to us here, Spirit of God, Spirit of Christ.
Amen.

CONFESSION

Dear God,
if ever we feel that we have nothing to confess, forgive us.
Not that we believe you always demand in us a sense of guilt,
or a fear of failure as though you are a harsh God.
Indeed, we come to you with faith in your unconditional grace.
We come to you as our loving parent
who understands all that we face in life,
and we thank you that this is so.

Silent reflection

We realize, O God, that because we are very human,
we sometimes think that we are clear about your will for us
when we have only seen part of the truth.
Our very humanness can lead us to believe
that we have your wisdom.
Forgive us if we have been tempted to believe that, O God.

Sometimes we judge the actions of others
because we think that our way is the only way,
and our understanding of things the only understanding.
If we have made those judgements,
forgive us, O God, and remind us of our fallibility
as very ordinary people.
For you and you alone are God, the all-knowing.
Amen.

ASSURANCE OF PARDON

In response to our confession,
Jesus Christ takes his place at the centre of our life,
full of forgiveness and grace,
full of understanding and the well-spring of our hope.
We are forgiven!
Thanks be to God.
Amen.

READINGS

Isaiah 43.16–21
Psalm 126
Philippians 3.4b–14
John 12.1–8

SERMON

84

HYMN

OFFERING

PRAYERS OF INTERCESSION

God, who is for all people,
who lives deeply within our life,
we pray today that we will be enlightened
so that we see what matters most in our efforts to participate
in the bringing in of your reign.

We pray for those whose lives have no room for imagination
because they have become engrossed in a narrow view of reality.
We pray for those who are oppressed
by people who only see their need of material things,
who are denied the subtle beauty,
the sweet smells, the wonder of magic sounds,
the delicacies of taste and touch
that many of us take for granted.

Silent reflection

We pray for our own life in your church,
that it may reflect the abundance
of all that you have prepared for us and for the world.
We pray that we will become the community
in which others will see the wholeness and beauty
of you, Jesus Christ.
We pray in your name,
Amen.

SENDING OUT

Go from this place in freedom and hope.
Go to pour perfume on a troubled world.
Go in faith to lift up the fullness of God's grace.

BLESSING

And may the God of love cover us with a robe of coloured life,
Christ Jesus spread bright flowers of grace beside our way
and the Spirit breathe gentleness in a cloud of hope around us.
Amen.

LITURGIES FOR
SPECIAL OCCASIONS

In the winters of life,
when the flowers and leaves have fallen by the wayside,
the stripped-back branches reach starkly towards the sky
and the roots cling to the earth and its rocky foundations
like a grip of hard-won faith,
there is God,
our company in the questioning,
the seeker after truth,
the passion in our indignation,
always gently, tenderly, holding us all in love.

A funeral for a baby or still-born child

Although a traditional funeral is often used for babies or still-born children, since the life with us was hardly begun and its passing is so painful and seemingly unjust, it seems to me that we need another type of ritual. This one has been used in relation to a number of babies who lived less than one day. It can be adjusted to be more focused on a child who never lived outside the womb.

For this service you will need

- *A beautiful centre for the focus using cloths*
- *Normally it is good to place the tiny casket on a central table*
- *A small candle and a taper for lighting it*
- *A bowl of water*
- *Baskets of small flowers which are placed on the table*

MUSIC

The casket is carried in

OPENING

We are here together to honour a small life,
the life of *Name*.
This loved child began its journey with us,
briefly and in fragility,
fleetingly but significantly.
We are here to grieve the passing of this life from our sight
and to stand near to *his/her* parents
as they remember this beginning of life
and its ending.

LIGHTING OF THE CANDLE

Let us light a tiny candle
as a symbol of this delicate life
which was unable to stay alight
and earthed among us.

The candle is lit

THE STORY

The story of the child is told – of its attempt to find and keep life

GIVING THANKS

Let us, in the silence,
give thanks to God for the life of this child.
Each moment of our journey with this life
is precious to us, O God.
Even as our thankfulness is overwhelmed with grief,
so that our joy is misted in pain,
we give you thanks for this life and all life.
Amen.

READINGS

Chosen Scripture passages

OR

A suggestion for another type of reading:

Your children are not your children.
They are the sons and daughters of Life's longing for itself.
They come through you but not from you,
and though they are with you yet they belong not to you.
You may give them your love but not your thoughts,

for they have their own thoughts.
You may house their bodies but not their souls,
for their souls dwell in the house of to-morrow,
which you cannot visit, not even in your dreams.
You may strive to be like them, but seek not to make them like
  you.
For life goes not backward nor tarries with yesterday.
(From Kahlil Gibran, *The Prophet*)

GRIEVING AND DREAMING

Our grieving lies like an unfilled space,
a painful place within our lives,
one which can never be truly filled by another.
Let us place a bowl of tears beside this tiny candle
as a symbol of our grieving.

The bowl is placed and a silence is kept

There were many things we wanted to give this child.
There were many dreams we had for our life together with
  him/her.
All these hopes and dreams we held for you, *Name.*
May the love we had prepared for you
reach out into the universe and touch your fragile spirit
held safe in the loving hands of God,
flying free, within us and beyond us.

As we hear this music, let us place flowers
around and over this small casket
as a cherishing of the precious little body which lies within it
and as symbols of the gifts we would have given this child.

Music while the people place the flowers

LETTING GO

This little life touched the earth very lightly,
leaving *his/her* fragile footsteps in our hearts
but unable to hold them to the ground.
His/Her spirit has now spread its wings
and joined the eternal life of God
in the mysteries of procreation,
beyond our understanding or our holding.

He/She did not leave us through lack of love,
nor because there was more that we should have done to sustain
　　life,
or because of our choices.
The miracle is that this brief time with us
was enough for the creation of love.

Our pain in letting go is the honouring of the love
which began in us
and which is now carried forth into all the winds of the skies
and the tides of the seas,
into the shining of the sun and the gentle light of the moon
travelling with the tiny life of *Name*,
in whatever form *he/she* now exists,
even if *his/her* existence only lies within us,
held close to God
and in the deepest reaches of our souls.

WE ARE HERE TOGETHER

Parents' names, you are not alone.
We are here together, ordinary human beings
who travel through life's pain and possibility,
holding on to each other with surprising courage and strength,
facing each day and each moment, whatever it may hold.
In your grieving we are with you.
In these next days we will be beside you.
You are surrounded and held by us all
and the tender love of God.
Receive our love.

THE FAREWELL

And now let us free this child to go on its next journey
towards God who is the centre of all compassion.
Let us leave *him/her* in this moment of loving.

A silence is kept

Go in peace, *Name.*
Travel safely in the loving hands of God,
who joins our hands in holding you in love as you go.

MOVING ON

This is not a forgetting, but a claiming of peace for the moving
    on.
This is not a leaving behind, but a carrying of this life
into new life for another day,
rather than a clinging to the life that could not be.
Let us go in freedom and hope,
in honour of the tiny special life which now journeys with us.
And may God, the loving parent, carry us into a new day,
Christ Jesus stretch out healing hands towards us
and the Spirit surround us with a cloud of grace.
Let us go from here in peace.
Amen.

MUSIC

AT THE CREMATORIUM

We now gather here to commit the body of *Name*
to the elements,
which are kind to us at the time of our death,
receiving us back into the cycle of living and dying,
growing and resting,
that all things may be eternally renewed.

A silence is kept

This body could never embrace all that is *Name*,
but was a holding place for *his/her* brief earthly journey,
and to be respected and honoured
because it gave us a glimpse of this loved child.
In the silence, let us pray or reflect
as we make our final farewell to *him/her*.

A silence is kept

COMMITTAL

We now commit the body of *Name*
to the life of the universe in its mystery and grace.
Go in peace, loved child.
Go in freedom towards new possibilities
and may the eternal love of God go with you.
Amen.

BLESSING

Go in peace,
free to hold each other in our grieving
and claiming the life that is still with us.
May the love in God surprise you on the way
and grace be found in many unexpected moments and people.
Amen.

A funeral for a person who has committed suicide

For this service you will need

- *A large bowl partly filled with water*
- *A large jug of water*
- *A basket of cut flowers*

OPENING

Dear friends,
we have come together
because we loved *Name*
as *son/daughter, brother/sister, family and friend.*
Here we will mourn *him/her* leaving us,
honour *his/her* life,
reverently farewell *his/her* body
and comfort each other.

We come believing that all human life is valuable,
that the truth and integrity and hopefulness
which resides in each life lives on.
We come, believing that *Name*'s life,
which we remember today
and for which we now experience great loss,
is joined in the eternal continuum of human endeavour
stretching into the past and into the future.
His/Her life was lived in its uniqueness with us
and has now passed into the ultimate community
of human existence and into the hands of God.

PRAYER

O God, at this moment,
as we come face to face with death,
especially this tragic death,

we have many feelings alongside our grief.
Please come close to us with your love,
travel with us into this harsh moment
and open our hearts to each other.
We ask it in the name of Jesus Christ,
who faced his own death and the death of a friend.
Amen.

Name chose the manner and the time of *his/her* dying
and this is hard for us to face.
In our grief, we ask ourselves whether,
if had we been different people,
or done something more for *him/her*,
he/she would have stayed longer with us
and chosen a gentler death.
There will never be enough tears to express our pain
as we recognize *his/her* pain at the ending of *his/her* life.
In our humanness, we are facing that there are times
when we will never have enough to offer
for the unlocking of life
and the sustaining of life in another.
We place this bowl of water,
the sign of our weeping,
at the centre of our life today.

The bowl is placed on the table

We may live with the questions for ever,
but the Gospel for us at this moment
is that all that is ever required of us
is that we do our best in loving each other
and in responding to each other's needs.
This we have done in all integrity,
both as a family and as a community of faith.
We are therefore called
to receive forgiveness if it is needed
and open our lives to the healing and comfort of God.
We are called to live our lives in peace
and trust in the grace of God

and the kindness of *Name himself/herself*,
a gift we all received in many forms
from *his/her* earliest years.
Let us now begin, in faith and hope,
to lay down the struggles of the past
and be open to the renewing of our lives.

A silence is kept

The gifts and graces which *Name* offered
must never be lost to us in the pain of *his/her* dying.
The creativity which *he/she* brought to us
in *his/her* life and relationships
lies now within our own lives
and travels into the future with us.
Our lives are more beautiful because we lived with *him/her*.

READINGS

REFLECTION

None of us knows the whole truth about what lies beyond death.
Christians believe that as we journey between life and death,
we are safe in the hands of an infinitely gracious God.
We believe that death invites us into total awareness
and to know with truth whether what we have valued
in ourselves has eternal value.
The God who stands with us at that moment
is the same God who was prepared to die in love for all
     humankind,
a God who has entered every struggle of our life with us
and who deeply understands the choices we have made.

REMEMBERING

As each person speaks about Name's *life, they place a flower in the bowl of water with the words:*

In Jesus Christ, the water of our tears
will become living water for the ongoing of life.

Let us pray or reflect in silence on this life and what it has meant to us:

Silent prayer/reflection

Thanks be to God for the gifts we have received in *Name*.

The minister/priest moves to the casket and placing a hand on it says:

Name, we will always wish you had stayed much longer with us
and that you had not chosen to die in this way,
but we will now set you free as you travel on into a new day.
We will always remember you
and all that you have given to us in your shortened life.
We will always value who you were for us.

To love someone is to risk the pain of parting.
Not to love is never to have lived.
The grief which we now experience is the honouring of our love.

Let us now in a quiet moment
make our farewell to *Name*.

Silence

PRAYER

For comfort and for all who grieve the loss of a loved one

COMMITTAL

And now let us commit *Name*'s body to the elements
which are gentle to us at the time of our death.
Ashes to ashes, dust to dust.
In the cycle of life and death the earth is replenished
and life is eternally renewed.

We send you out now, *Name*,
to go safely into the gentle hands of God
for this next part of your journey.
May a greater wholeness and fullness of life
be waiting for you.
Our love goes with you.
May you now find peace.
Amen.

BLESSING AND DISMISSAL

Even as we grieve this loss,
let us commit ourselves to the comfort of those who miss *Name*
    most,
especially . . .
Let us surround them with our love
and pray for the comfort of God.

And now let us go into the world,
glad that we have loved,
free to weep for the one we have lost,
free to hold each other in our human frailty,
empowered to live life to the full
and to affirm the hope of human existence.
And may God be our company,
Christ Jesus walk before us
and the Spirit surround us with a cloud of grace.
Amen.

Two rituals for the disposal of ashes

Many people these days hold the ashes of a family member or friend after cremation and sometimes like to have a brief ritual around their scattering or burial. These two rituals are examples of the way this could be done. Usually a special place is chosen that was precious to the person who died, or is precious to those who grieve for the loss of that person. Most people choose a public place in the countryside, in a park or by the sea, but others prefer a place closer to home, a private place.

Anyone can lead these brief rituals – often it is better to have someone outside the immediate family so that those closest to the person can be truly free to participate without undue responsibility.

For these rituals you will need

- *Whatever you decide should accompany the ashes or be placed over them, such as flowers.*

A ritual for the burial of ashes

WE ARE HERE

We are here because *Name* asked this of us.
This was a special place for *her/him*,
one which carried memories of life which were precious.
Let us remember.

A silence is kept as people remember or brief memories about the place and its connection with the person are shared

Here we will bury *her/his* ashes
as part of our farewell
and as a sign of the setting free of *Name*
to leave us and enter *her/his* next journey,
whatever that may be.

100

OR

WE ARE HERE

We are here because this is a special place for us,
a place which will always carry for us memories of *Name*,
the one we loved.
Let us remember.

*A silence is kept as people remember or brief memories about the
place and its connection with the person are shared*

Today we will make this a place which will always be sacred for
    us
because it holds the ashes of our family member and friend.
This will be part of our farewell
and a sign of the setting free of *Name*
to leave us and enter *her/his* next journey,
whatever that may be.

RETURNING TO THE EARTH

We will now make a welcoming place for *her/his* ashes,
not because we believe that *Name herself/himself* is now here,
because *her/his* spirit could never be contained in these ashes.
The true life of *Name* has now joined the greater life of God.
We care for these ashes as a mark of love and respect
for the part of human life which always returns to the earth
in a cycle of renewal,
which makes its small contribution to the future of the planet.
We will do it as those who are now prepared to let *Name* go,
even as we grieve.

Let us now prepare this place for *Name*'s ashes
and place them there with love and care.

A hole is dug in the earth and the ashes are placed

Before we cover them,
let us hear a poem
and/or some words which we want said
in remembering and celebration.

Readings, poems and/or thoughts are shared

THE COVERING

Let us now cover the ashes
and prepare them for our leaving,
placing flowers over the earth
as a sign of the love we have for *Name*
and for this earth and its beauty.

The ashes are gently covered and flowers placed over the earth

SENDING OUT

May the gentle rain visit this place with its greening of life,
may the winds of freedom move in delight among the trees
        around it
and connect its breathing and growing with the spirit of *Name.*
May the sun light it and warm it with love every day,
just as we have loved our *husband, father, partner, daughter,
        sister, aunt, friend (as appropriate)*
and as *she/he* has loved us.
Let us go in peace.

A ritual for the scattering of ashes

WE ARE HERE

We are here because *Name* asked this of us.
This was a special place for *her/him*,

one which carried memories of life which were precious.
Let us remember.

*A silence is kept as people remember or brief memories about the
place and its connection with the person are shared*

Here we will scatter *her/his* ashes
as part of our farewell
and as a sign of the setting free of *Name*
to leave us and enter *her/his* next journey,
into the hands of God.

OR

WE ARE HERE

We are here because this is a special place for us,
a place which will always carry for us memories of *Name*,
the one we loved.
Let us remember.

*A silence is kept as people remember or brief memories about the
place and its connection with the person are shared*

Today we will make this a place which will always be sacred for
    us
because it receives the ashes of our family member and friend.
This will be part of our farewell
and a sign of the setting free of *Name*
to leave us and enter *her/his* next journey,
whatever that may be.

SCATTERING THE ASHES

Let us look at the beauty of this place
which will now receive the ashes of *Name*.
It waits to receive them as a gift for its future life.
It will be the joining of this one life with the life of the universe.

We will scatter these ashes
as those who are now prepared to let *Name* go,
even as we grieve.

Before we do this,
let us hear a poem
and/or some words which we want said
in remembering and celebration.

Readings or poems and/or thoughts are shared

We will scatter these ashes
as those who are now prepared to let *Name* go,
even as we grieve.
We will let *her/him* go so that *she/he* will return to us in a new
    way,
as gentle memory, as unexpected presence,
as love and laughter in many forms.

A silence is kept

We will scatter these ashes
and send *Name* on the great journey into universal life,
life which is as free as these ashes floating in the air,
one with the wind and as light as sunshine.
We now send *Name* into life
which is as strong as our hopes,
and as lively and as wide as the sea.

Our love gathers around these ashes as they go,
not because they could ever hold the whole being of *Name*,
whose life and spirit
could never be contained in a few small ashes,
but because they are small echoes of the one we have loved,
and go on loving.

The ashes are scattered

Travel safely and well, *Name*.

We will follow you with flowers,
to go with you on your way
and in celebration of our love for you,
and who you will always be for us.

The flowers are thrown

SENDING OUT

May the gentle rain visit this place with its greening of life,
may the winds of freedom move in delight among the trees
    around it
and connect its breathing and growing with the spirit of *Name*.
May the sun light it and warm it with love every day,
just as we have loved our *husband, father, partner, daughter,*
    sister, aunt, friend (as appropriate)
and as *she/he* has loved us.
Let us go in peace.

OR

May the tides of the sea carry our loved one with joy
on the peaks of its waves,
and in its surges of passionate life.
May the sun on the water be bright with hopes for all that is to
    come
and the calm moon cherish all life with gentleness.
May the waters of the seas move across the face of the earth with
    love every day,
just as we have loved our *husband, father, partner, daughter,*
    sister, aunt, friend (as appropriate)
and as *she/he* has loved us.
Let us go in peace.

Creating a space for friendship
Celebrating unity in diversity of faiths

This service was first created when there was a time of rejection of Muslim people in Australian society after terrorist attacks around the world.

For this service you will need:

- *The church or hall set up with chairs around a space*
- *Representatives from the diverse groups present prepared to name themselves and their origins/faiths and form the circle of diversity*
- *Cut flowers in a basket*
- *Children invited in advance to do drawings or paintings about friendship*
- *If possible, a meal to share*

MUSIC

WELCOME

Welcome to all present.

GREETING

With respect and gratitude for the original custodians of this land
    (*if appropriate*),
we are gathered together today to affirm in hope and faith
that we can create a space for friendship and respect
across our different religions,
across race and culture,
across political divides and painful histories.

This is who we are,
many people of great diversity,
one community in the unity of humankind.

*Invite representatives of the diversity present to form a circle in the
space and name themselves, e.g.*

I am *Name* and I am an Indonesian Australian and a Muslim.
I am *Name* and I am a Scottish Australian and a Christian.

SONG

GRIEVING

In the centre of this space is terrible silence of death and
     wounding,
the sounds of weeping and pain
which arise from the violences around the world
and in the lives of all who suffer.
We also hold in special care (*name any particular situations*)
We will bring the lament of the people into this space.
We will surround the grieving with our loving care.

LAMENTS FROM VARIOUS TRADITIONS

*Any children present are invited to help make a circle of flowers
around the circle, the space for the grieving*

LET US REMEMBER TRUST

When we begin to destroy each other
in lack of compassion and rejection,
in abuse and harassment,
in prejudice and hate,
in violence and war,

we end the childlike innocence which is our birthright.
Through the eyes of our children of today, let us remember trust.
Let us remember hope and the dream of human friendship.

Invite children to bring their pictures or poems and stand in the circle holding them

THE SACRED TASK

The sacred task for adults is to honour the hopes of all the
    world's children
for their safety and security,
to care for them gently and deeply – in body, mind, heart and
    soul.

The children are invited to place their paintings within the circle of flowers

What will the world hold in trust for its children?
What will we create here in this space
and in our country?
Let us hear the call from our sacred texts.

READINGS FROM THE SACRED TEXTS

About love for one another

CELEBRATION

We will sing and dance this hope, we will create our poetry
to celebrate the new possibilities for humankind.

Songs and/or dances from various traditions

THE NEW COMMUNITY

Let us imagine the new community of humankind,
all peoples living in compassion and respect for each other,
an end to violence and hate,
the bringing in of equality and justice.
a great circle of friendship around the world beginning here.

The diverse people gather in a circle in the space again

In awe, in silence, let us reflect on this new world.

A silence is kept

After the silence, let us hear some words of encouragement

REFLECTIONS FROM VARIOUS LEADERS

LET US PRAY

Let us place around this dream
the power of our prayers,
our ways of connecting with love beyond ourselves,
with the energy for good at the centre of all creation.
As we do this, let us feel the joining of our friendship around this
    space
with the heart of the universe.

Prayers from the various traditions in their own languages

LET US ACT

Each of us is a participant in the formation of the future.
Some of us will do small things and others larger,
but each will offer what we can in our daily lives.
Let us begin now:

Here are some ideas for our time together over lunch:

- In this corner, some of us may like to begin a petition where we call upon our leaders to carry us forward into a friendlier world.
- Over here, some of us may simply like to meet other people who are here and share stories of where we have come from and our life experience.
- In that corner, some may want to talk together about ideas for a possible family day which may happen in the future.
- Others still may simply want to join in the laying out of the food we are about to share by going over to that corner and preparing the tables.

SONG

GO IN PEACE

Before we move, let us stand a little closer together
and look around the room at the faces around the space:
let us see the life that is written there,
see the beauty of the diversity of people,
see our strength and our vulnerability.
Together we will create a new place here and a new world to
    come.

Brief silence

We will begin with the sharing of food.

Food is carried into the centre and lifted high

We are thankful for this food which we will share together in
    friendship.
Go in peace.

MUSIC

Peace liturgy for Palm Sunday

PREPARATION

People are invited to bring branches from a tree common to their area.

OPENING

On this day, of all days,
we celebrate the Christ who comes in courage,
riding in glorious liberty between the lines of our life,
towards every possible future,
celebrating, challenging, hoping against hope,
carried on the back of faith
and claiming the ground for good.
Salute this Christ today,
the one who comes into our midst
on a costly and holy journey,
the Prince of Peace.

WE ARE GATHERED

We are gathered here today
to take our stand against war,
to make that known to our leaders and the world
and to pray for peace in our times.

As we do this, we bring together
the energy of our own love for the world,
in all its complex struggles,
and the energy of God, who is the centre of all life,
eternal love, eternal peace, eternal justice.

LET US REMEMBER

Let us remember the first Palm Sunday:
Let us imagine the people
who hoped for a different world in their day
and who saw in Jesus the source of that hope.

They were people just like us:
cheering on the good one day
and betraying it on the next,
longing for peace and justice one moment,
but losing faith, or growing tired in the struggle,
long before that peace and justice is achieved.
Let us, in the silence, remember our humanness
and invite the forgiveness of God.

A silence is kept

ASSURANCE

The God of peace and justice
is also the God of grace.
We are forgiven.
Thanks be to God.

PATHWAYS FOR PEACE

The people of the first Palm Sunday
took the branches of a common tree
in their part of the world
and made a pathway
for the journeying of the Christ.

We, too, have brought our branches.
Let us, where we are, turn towards each other
and make small pathways between us
as we lay our branches on the ground.

112

The people do so

Let us hold the silence
as we grieve the violence in our world,
the lack of compassion, the moves into war,
and then receive the prayers from church leaders
for peace in our time.

A silence is held, broken by the prayers of church leaders

Now, let us return to the silence
and imagine that these, our small pathways of branches,
have become the pathway to peace
through which the Christ will travel.

*A silence is kept, broken by a single voice singing a suitable hymn
or song*

RIDE ON, PRINCE OF PEACE

Ride on, ride on, Prince of Peace, Christ of Justice.
Ride on to reign over all that destroys and wounds the world,
all that abuses and exploits the weak,
all that crushes joy in dearly held and trembling hopes,
all that violates sacred trust when it is born among us.
Ride on, Prince of Peace,
for we pray in your name, Jesus Christ,
Amen.

LET US GO

As we are sent on to be the people of God,
let us hold our branches high,
for the greenness will rise from the ground,
following the footsteps of Christ.

The people do so

Let us go in faith,
for the Christ is walking ahead of us on the way.

BLESSING

And may the Prince of Peace reign in all the earth,
God the Creator place a loving hand beneath us
and the Holy Spirit surround us and heal us.
Amen.

An insert for a marriage of people who have been divorced

Sometimes when people marry for a second time they feel as though there should be some recognition that they are about to make new vows, rather than first vows. There are sometimes children of first marriages involved. This insertion was created for such an occasion.

To be inserted after 'The declaration of purpose' in the marriage service:

In human life, we enter vulnerable journeys of commitment
and hopes which are sometimes not sustained.
We make our vows in faith
and we walk through the valleys of the death of those vows.
Often we do not know whether the journey we chose
was mistaken in its beginnings, or mistaken in its endings.
The endings of a marriage are not made lightly, but with grieving.

Whatever the truth which lies within our human failure,
we know that the gospel frees us to begin life afresh,
to make new vows in celebration of the promises of God
and the miracles of grace which are offered to us through Jesus
    Christ
and in the love of each other.

For *Name* and *Name* this is a second marriage.
They wish to make their vows to each other today,
and before their friends and family,
with an honest recognition of all that has gone before.
They celebrate the grace that is present here
in their children and in their previous partners.

**To be inserted, if requested, as an addition to the section which
calls upon all present to uphold those being married and to
offer their support:**

Addressed to the previous partner/s:
Will you, who have shared the lives of *Name* and *Name* in
marriage,
and who have now, after the closure of that relationship,
joined these people as friends for their future,
support them in the upholding of their vows to each other
and celebrate their marriage?
We will.

Addressing children of the previous marriages:
Will you, the children of *Name* and *Name*,
celebrate the parents you have always known,
trusting in their love for you,
and receive with hope a new parent
with whom to share your life journeys?
We will.

The winters of our days

A liturgy for the naming and receiving of our hard questions for God

'and the leaves of the tree are for the healing of the nations'
(Revelation 22.2)

Often in the church, we are not very good at sharing our hard questions for God. They are more likely to be asked outside the church. This liturgical framework is not inviting the giving of answers but the respectful and brave sharing of questions. People are often very relieved to be able to do this.

For this liturgy you will need

- *Pieces of paper and pens for people to take as they enter, or on the tables the people are to gather around*
- *A flat bowl of earth*
- *A basket of various leaves*

OPENING

In the winters of life,
when the flowers and leaves have fallen by the wayside,
the stripped-back branches reach starkly towards the sky
and the roots cling to the earth and its rocky foundations
like a grip of hard-won faith,
there is God,
our company in the questioning,
the seeker after truth,
the passion in our indignation,
always gently, tenderly, holding us all in love.

In the silence,
let us place this day and all our journeying
along the pathways of life and trembling faith,
into the hands of God.

A silence is kept

IN FAITH WE COME

In faith, O God,
we dare to bring to you the doubts, the questions,
the anxieties, the angers and the pain
which are part of our journey through life.
We place them all in truth into your hands
for your care and compassion.

Silent reflection

We are sorry if we have kept them from you,
as though we are afraid of your judgement,
or our own lack of answers,
which we fear may be your lack of answers
and which may shake our faith.

Silent reflection

In faith we come, as we are,
as we have been and as we may be,
for you are our God
and we are your people.
In the name of Jesus Christ,
Amen.

NAMING THE QUESTIONS

Let us in this time together reflect on our hard questions for God,
writing them on the paper provided. Then, if you wish to do so,
share your hard questions for God with the people near to you.
Let us not feel that we need to try to answer the questions. Let
us rather just listen respectfully.

The people do so

READING

Revelation 22.1–5

WE PRAY

Just as the night kindly covers the earth with its restfulness,
and the tree of life waits quietly and hopefully for the day,
so we rest in your love, O God.
Silent prayer

We gather up the restless questioning,
the painful grieving and wounding,
the stressed striding of our lives
and the struggling aches of ageing,
and place them under the leaves of the tree
for your healing, wisdom and grace.

*The people place their prayers and questions on the earth and
cover them with the leaves*

We leave them there for the morning of our days,
not grasping for neat solutions or quick and easy answers,
but as a sign of our honest travelling in life
and of our commitment to live
with its mysteries and silences
in mutual compassion and searching.
**We will watch for the buds of new possibilities
and keep the faith for each other and with each other
until the dawning of deeper understanding.**

Silent reflection

We know that you will never leave us alone, loving God.
**Help us in our times of unbelief,
lead us to your living water
and call us to the shade of peace under the tree of life.
Amen.**

SENDING OUT

Go out in faith into the world which struggles to believe.
Go in peace to walk the grand and glorious way of Jesus Christ.

BLESSING

And may the winters of life
be filled with the warm light of the Spirit,
the promise of God be around you
like the emerging of spring,
and the Christ be discovered waiting for you
at every bend in the road.
Amen.

In the beginning

A service for the beginning of a task or the beginning of a year

For this service you will need

- *A candle and the means of lighting it*
- *A long flowing cloth*
- *A basket of flowers*

CALL TO WORSHIP

In the beginning
there was nothing but God,
and from that nothingness,
arose the miracle of universal life.

In our beginnings,
as we enter a new year,
God lies in the empty spaces,
bringing light to old things.

The candle is lit

God goes on,
spreading life beyond where we have been.

A cloth is spread from the table and down the centre

God is always creating the wonder of newness for us.
Let us worship God.

HYMN

CONFESSION

All of us carry with us past experiences,
past failures or mistakes,
which lie like burdens in our lives.
All of us have histories in relationships,
things which we wish we had not done or said,
or which should have happened, but never did,
and which will not enhance our future together.
In the silence, let us reflect
on things we would rather not carry into this year.

A silence is kept

Take all these our burdens into your life, O God.
**We lay them down in faith
for healing, forgiveness, re-creation and release.
Amen.**

ASSURANCE

Hear the word of God for us:
'See the former things have come to pass
and new things I now declare;
before they break from the bud, I announce them to you.'
Rise up and live in hope.
Grace is ours this day.
Amen.

READINGS

Isaiah 42.5–9
John 1.1–5

SERMON

AFFIRMATION OF FAITH

Let us affirm our faith together:
**In this new beginning,
in faith we claim our life together,
full with the sharing of our gifts,
and the gifts of God,
empty of pride because we stand before God's holiness,
searching in our journey towards deeper truth,
empowered by the life of the Spirit among us
and the friendship of Jesus Christ.**

**In hope we commit ourselves to (*the project is named*),
to a greater dream for the new year
and the grand adventure of being your people.**

INVITING THE CREATIVITY OF GOD

God who is our Creator,
we ask you to go on creating new things in us.
Remembering your promise of buds
which will blossom freshly in our life,
we ask for the gifts we need as we begin this year:

*The people take a flower, place it on the cloth, and name the gift
they believe is needed*

Nothing is impossible with you, O God.
**Take all that we are and add to us your creative life,
that we may be part of your faithful community here.**

Then, O God, widen our horizons
so that we may take our rightful place as citizens of the world,
expanding your loving and just life beyond these boundaries
until the whole creation sings in joy with the life of your Spirit.
**We pray in the name of Jesus Christ,
Amen.**

HYMN

SENDING OUT

Go in peace into the tasks and relationships which lie ahead.
Go in faith because you never travel alone.
God is with us and we are with each other.

BLESSING

And may you tread in the footsteps of the Christ,
safely walking on the rock which is our God
and covered by the warm bright wings of the Holy Spirit.
Amen.

A liturgy for weeknight meetings

Christ be with you.
And also with you.

OPENING

We are the people of God:
called this day, as on every day,
to walk in brave faith
towards each other and the world.

We are the people of God:
called in freedom and in hope,
with tears and with laughter,
to travel deeply into the life of God
and the humble human journey.

CONFESSION AND ASSURANCE

We will never be who we would long to be.
We will never reach the heights and depths,
the measure of grace or the perfecting of truth
which lies in the God we serve.
But this will not separate us
from the love of God in Christ Jesus,
the renewing Parent and Creator
and the eternal gifts of the Holy Spirit.
This is the faith we affirm,
Amen.

READING

Maybe the Gospel reading for the week

RESPONSE

In response to the word,
let us pray for others and ourselves.
**In prayer we join our love and care together
and expand it with the universal love of God.**

Let us name before God those whose lives and situations
cry out for our concern at this time:

The people bring their prayers

Prayer is a sign of our commitment
to a new heaven and a new earth
and the company of God in that transforming task.
**Walk before us, Jesus Christ,
cover us with your warm wings as we go, loving Parent,
and be our inspiration and wisdom, Holy Spirit.
Amen.**

BLESSING

Go into this hour in peace and courage.
And may the Holy God open new possibilities before us,
Christ Jesus sit at the table beside us
and the Spirit dance on in the passion of life.
Amen.

Laying the Word on the Earth

A prayer for the Bible

I now lay the Word of God on the earth,
the earth with its patterns of beauty and grace,
in its dryness and its waters of life,
its wilderness and its vulnerability,
its fragile light
and its calm darkness.

There may it struggle with the stored death
and stored life.
There may it dance and play,
and discover the deep connection
between the profound and the absurd.

Some of it will die.
Some of it will blossom.
Much of it will stay on the ground
and release seeds for the future
as it touches the life of its Creator.

We lay the Word of God, the Bible, on the earth.
May our own lives bring it to life
and may God travel in its every journey among us.
Amen.

Remembering the donation of an organ by someone you love

A meditation

I will remember you with love as you lived –
part of my life, part of my loving.
I see you now, whole and breathing,
your body carrying your mind and heart and soul,
God's gift to us, uniquely with us,
all with us,
changing us because you were among us,
important to us.

Silent reflection

For those who live with the decision of the donor:

I will remember you with love,
even as you decided to give this gift from yourself,
this gift of yourself.
My heart wonders whether you ever knew what it would mean?
My soul cries a little,
because sometimes it feels that we lost a part of you somewhere,
even as we honour your offering of life to another,
a God-like gift.
Sometimes the images of that gap in your body are painful to me.
Sometimes I wanted to say, 'No!' and, 'Have you thought of us?'

On some days I wonder whether the one who now lives through
    you
is grateful enough.
I want that person and those who love that person to be very,
    very grateful
and I will never know whether they are, or not.
But, deep down, I believe that they are grateful,
that your gift was received with tears of hope
and that God is honouring your gift.

There are days when I look at people as they walk by me
and ask myself, 'Could it be that person?'
Does that person look worthy of a special gift?
Is this person different because you lived and died?
I am not sure that I want to know
because I would be tempted to see if I like them.
I remember your kindness of heart and the essence of you
which still lives on complete in some sure way,
the gap in your body filled by the grace of your soul.
I know you did it for yourself, your own completeness of living.
I try to hold on to that, to see that gathered into the mystery of
    God.
I do try to hold on to that, as you call me to do.

Silent reflection

For those who made the decision on behalf of the donor:

Engrained in my heart and mind for ever
will live the moment of decision to give part of you to another.
In our time of loss it eased us a little to know
that something of you had the power to survive and to bring life
    to another.
And yet, in the deeps of the night the murky fears visit me still –
were you really dead?
What if there was the possibility of some miracle
waiting around the next corner,
and we denied you that deliverance?
What if your soul was still attached to your body
and felt a violation as part of you was taken,
and you knew we had asked that of you?
What if you live on in another place, another generation,
and will always long for what is no longer there for you?
What if you never forgive us for doing this to you,
because you would have chosen differently?
Sometimes this is added to my grieving for you,
the one I loved,
added like a weight.
And then I remember who you were
and who we were together.

I hold on to that,
because you lived with generosity,
you related to us with grace in life.
I will trust that you will not have changed in death.
I will trust that God gathers your completeness
and holds you in loving embrace for ever.
This I believe. This I will believe.

Silent reflection

So, how will I hold you now?
How will I see you in my mind's eye?
How will I carry you on into the future?

Silent reflection

I will remember you with love as you died –
still part of my life, part of my loving.
I see you now as I saw you then,
as you moved into the mystery of spaces beyond my reaching,
except as I remember you in my heart,
except as I feel the loss of you in life and the pain of you in
     death.

Silent reflection

I will remember you with honour,
as your body gives life to another,
life which cost you some of yourself,
life which gives a gracious gift in the face of death.

Silent reflection

I will restore your wholeness on this day.
I will bring you into a healed place in my heart and soul,
holding you again with me, cradling your life in mine.
Your body is transformed in God's universal creation
of giving new life from the earth, from the fire, from the waters,
from the mystery of the seed
which breaks open and gives as it dies to itself.

Silent reflection

You are never lost to me.
You are never less than yourself to me.
You are the grace which offers to us all
a vision of the generosity, the loving kindness,
the faithful commitment to a human community
which is carried into eternity.

Silent reflection

I will remember you.

Honouring the receiving of an organ donation

A meditation

My heart leaps within me, my body sings in gratitude for a gift of
    life!
Life given by another, life as gift of God.

I remember, with respect, the journey that now lies in the past –
the wondering, the waiting,
the hard moments of lack of good future,
an empty deadliness within,
the wondering if God was really with me at all.

Silent reflection

I remember the waking with anticipation,
as if that was to be the day
and the sleeping at the end of the day when nothing had changed.

Silent reflection

I remember looking at the world
as though it should somehow know
that such a modest gift would save me,
a gift of something which would die without my receiving it,
a gift which nobody seemed to have for the giving.
I read of deaths
and wonder if there was ever a thought for my need,
such a small thing it sometimes seemed,
such an obvious possibility.
And yet the days went by,
the world went by,
sometimes God's love went by,
my silent hopefulness went by.
People died and were born.
Sometimes others were given the vital offering of life,
and there I was, still waiting,
waiting for ever, it seemed,
waiting for ever.

Silent reflection

And then the day,
the precious call which gave me the offering of life,
the trembling of my body, heart and soul,
as I hurried towards hope
as though it was a dream and might not stay long enough
for me to arrive to receive it.

Silent reflection

And now, I live.
I live because someone else has died
and in the dying has given a costly gift to carry me into a new
    future.
I live as though on borrowed time
and yet no one asks for its returning.

Silent reflection

I cannot bring to my eye the giver
because I will never know a name or see a face,
or ask what it meant or even what it means
to that person's ongoing – if there is one?

Is there someone now transported into universal life,
held close in the arms of God,
who carries a small emptiness within
which can only be filled by my gratitude?
Is there someone who is forever linked to my life
in the mystery of human continuity,
in the wonder of the unknown existence beyond this earth?
Do they hear my voice as I try to find words to say what I feel?
Do they see my tears of gratitude?
Do they follow my journey a little as though to see how I travel
    on?

Silent reflection

Will I ever have moments when I am not completely my own,
or have I been set free to receive this gift
and make it a true part of me?
I would like that to be so,
I would pray that it is so.
Maybe that is part of the wonder of the gift?
I will believe that it is.
May God give me wisdom as I live with this gift.

Silent reflection

And then I remember those who still wait.
I was one of them, a community of longing,
a community of patience and impatience.
What if they think I have been favoured?
Some of them have been waiting longer than I did.
Have I been favoured in some way I do not recognize?
Is there something that I should be doing to deserve this gift
when others still wait?
Deal gently with me, God.
I am no more than I ever was.

Is there a God somewhere who expects me to earn this gift,
to repay it in some way?
Am I good enough to receive this gift,
when others don't have it?
Will I be able to look them in the face?
Should I share my joy with them,
or will it add to their sorrow?
Sometimes these questions stay with me
and filter through my delight
like small dark threads of anxiety.
Maybe I can look at them safely
and know that some are real concerns and some are old
     hauntings about a harsh God.
Maybe I can gently lay them down
and convert them into care for those who still wait,
and my freedom to celebrate something which will never be
     deserved
but is given in the generous hope that I will take it and fully live.

Silent reflection

And now I remember those who loved the giver of the gift,
those who watched the dying and the giving,
and let the loved one leave them with a bestowed inheritance of
     life
which they may not have expected.
I remember them with gratitude.
I honour their new journey, which is now forever connected with
     my own.
I give thanks to the giver and those who loved that person.
Thanks to the giver!
Thanks for my new life.
Thanks be to God.